S0-FSS-620

Bibliographical Procedures & Style

A Manual for Bibliographers in the Library of Congress

By BLANCHE PRICHARD McCRUM
and HELEN DUDENBOSTEL JONES

THE LIBRARY OF CONGRESS
REFERENCE DEPARTMENT • GENERAL REFERENCE AND BIBLIOGRAPHY DIVISION
WASHINGTON : 1954

L. C. Card 54-60016

For sale by the Superintendent of Documents, U. S. Government Printing Office, Washington 25, D. C. - Price 65 cents

CONTENTS

PREFACE

The present publication has three main purposes. First, it suggests methods of planning and carrying through a bibliographical project. Second, it provides a style manual of forms of entry developed by the General Reference and Bibliography Division, through the adaptation of rules followed by catalogers of the Library's collections. Third, in response to numerous requests from students and scholars, it makes currently available a manual used by Library of Congress bibliographers. An earlier guide, prepared by Mortimer Taube and Helen F. Conover, was entitled Manual for Bibliographers in the Library of Congress (Washington, 1944. 28 p.). The stock of that pioneer brochure was soon exhausted, and up to this time the publication has not been superseded. In summary, Bibliographical Procedures and Style is intended as a handbook of standard practices and techniques, so far as standardization is possible or desirable.

Among the more important individual aims of the publication is that of emphasizing the unity of principles underlying the preparation of bibliographical entries and of Library of Congress catalog cards. By following the rules provided for this purpose the bibliographer not only may make productive use of printed catalog cards for recording citations, but may also apply the same principles when referring to articles in periodicals and to other publications not individually recorded in the catalogs of the Library of Congress. Certain departures from cataloging rules also must be made by the bibliographer, because the physical form, scope, and purpose of bibliographies and card catalogs are not identical. These necessary adaptations have been spelled out in succeeding pages.

It is perfectly true, moreover, that factors such as the emergence of new types of materials, requirements of potential users of the bibliography, or the overall purpose for which the work is undertaken may suggest departures from previously accepted bibliographical norms. In such situations it is by no means the purpose of the Library of Congress to force its bibliographers into undesirable conformity, to suggest the application of rules that are not relevant, or to relieve them of the obligation to make innovations and changes when these are required. If, however, new principles are to be substituted for those previously established, the burden of proof rests on the innovator. It is essential, therefore, to provide for his use a manual which records standards currently acceptable within the institution. Should departures from these standards be in order, guidance may be obtained from the selected list of references in Appendix F and from Miss Kinney's detailed survey of sources of information on bibliographical citations in the major subject fields.[1/]

[1/] Kinney, Mary R. Bibliographical style manuals; a guide to their use in documentation and research. Chicago, Association of College and Reference Libraries, 1953. 21 p. (ACRL monographs, no. 8) Z674.A75, no. 8

No effort is made here to trespass on the preserves of the specialist. Descriptive bibliography of rare books is left to experts in that field. Special forms of entry for the literature of law, music, technical scientific reports, and patents are not within the scope of the present study. Nonbook materials, such as prints, photographs, maps, and phonorecords also have been omitted from consideration until bibliographers in the various specialized disciplines have had an opportunity to determine the value to them of a general manual.

Comments and suggestions based on the use of Bibliographical Procedures and Techniques are cordially invited and will be given serious consideration in future revisions.

Burton W. Adkinson
Director, Reference Department

PART ONE

BIBLIOGRAPHICAL PROCEDURES

I. PLANNING THE BIBLIOGRAPHY

The exploitation of each opportunity to make a bibliographical contribution is limited by such factors as availability of funds, the character of institutional holdings, the presence on the staff of qualified bibliographers, and the time that may be devoted to the work. The audience to be served and the purpose to be accomplished are also basic considerations. Obviously, therefore, the initiation of a bibliographical project must receive exceedingly careful consideration before decisions concerning it are reached. Reaching such conclusions and planning the bibliography, if the undertaking has been justified, cannot, however, be achieved by following precise rules. Even within one library considerations that must be taken into account vary from project to project. Nevertheless, in order that so essential a part of bibliographical work as its planning may not be left in a state of continual improvisation, suggestions for systematic planning are provided here. These must be adapted to fit individual cases as may be necessary; but in general five important stages of planning may be described as follows: (1) the preliminary survey by the bibliographer; (2) the bibliographer's report; (3) consideration of the report; (4) the work sheet of essential information; and (5) the progress report in relation to revision of plans.

A. The Preliminary Survey by the Bibliographer.

The first aim of the bibliographer assigned to the project is that of gaining an overall view of the undertaking. Next, he hopes to establish the importance, or lack of it, of the whole idea. And finally, if his findings are favorable to it, he expects to make a blueprint of a plan that will result in a finished bibliography. Methods to be used at this stage of the work are suggested under Investigation of the Literature, a section of the manual in which Procedures are discussed in some detail. Emphasis should be given immediately, however, to the fact that the survey is preliminary only in the sense that it comes before the actual identification, selection, and description of items to be included in a completed bibliography. In reality, it is expected to be final with reference to equally important parts of the work. Among these may be mentioned the acquisition of adequate knowledge of the content and the logical subdivisions of the subject, gained from intensive study of pertinent literature, and from aids to research in the field. Conclusions also derived from such a study relate to the suitability of the library collections for the kind of exploration that is indicated, details that may call for revision of the original idea, and reliable estimates of the essential scope of the bibliography. It is during this phase of the work that the bibliographer's subject specialization in the sources of documentary knowledge is put immediately to productive use to provide sound judgments of the worth and the requirements of the whole assignment. At this point his knowledge, professional skill, and initiative perhaps receive their most rigorous test. Consequently he organizes the preliminary survey by preparing a systematic guide in the form of a detailed outline of points to be covered. Experience in the Library of Congress suggests the usefulness of the following checklist, to be amplified as required by the character of the particular subject.

1. Evidence of the importance of the subject with respect to bibliographical development:
   a. Extent of its literature.
   b. Currency of interest in it.
   c. Status of bibliographies in the field (past, present, projected).

2. Availability of aids to research, e.g., encyclopedias, guides, manuals, indexes, abstracting services, journals, theses, book reviews, monumental collections, standard texts, etc.

3. Indications of types of significant material with respect to:
   a. Languages.
   b. Periods.
   c. Countries or regions.
   d. Forms, e.g., books, official documents, serials, articles, pamphlets, etc., as well as phonorecords, maps, microfilms, and other nonbook materials.

4. Adequacy of subject headings: (a) in the card catalogs of the library, for delimiting the topic and showing its relation to other subjects; and (b) in indexes and other publications using different terminology.

5. Necessity of supplementing approach through the card catalogs by means of:
   a. The shelflist.
   b. Direct search of the shelves.
   c. Published lists and catalogs.

6. Coverage of the subject provided by the collections of the library.

7. Facilities for more productive work in other libraries and special collections.

8. Advice resulting from personal consultations with specialists in the field and with the instigators of the bibliographical project.

When the bibliographer has worked through his checklist of fundamental considerations, he is in a position to describe his findings in a report.

B. The Bibliographer's Report.

The main purposes of such a report are three: (1) to record, in a brief and systematic form, the significant preliminary conclusions of the bibliographer; (2) to provide the necessary data for decisions with respect to the further prosecution of the project; and (3) to furnish guidance for associates or successors that may be assigned to the project if it is approved.

Details upon which recommendations in the report also may be expected at this time include the definition and limitation to be placed upon the subject of the bibliography, the title that will best express its purpose and content, the scope of the work, the extent, whether inclusive or selective, a tentative estimate of entries to be made, and the time and personnel required to accomplish the assignment completely or partially. Possibly certain stylistic matters, also, may be clarified by this time, so that the bibliographer may wish to recommend the amount of detail with which entries should be prepared, variations in bibliographic style required by types of materials to be cited, and the arrangement of entries best suited to the purpose of the bibliography.

The formulation of these conclusions and recommendations, documented by brief statements of significant facts, constitutes the report, which then becomes the agenda of a conference to determine the future of the project. Participants in the conference are the supervisory official (or officials) with responsibility for decision concerning bibliographic projects, the bibliographer, and possibly subject specialists to act as consultants.

C. Consideration of the Report.

When the weight of the evidence produced by the bibliographer in his report is conclusively against undertaking the project, the work of the conference is finished as soon as debatable points have been clarified. If, on the contrary, the report indicates that modifications of the original idea are in order, the bibliographer probably will be asked to explore these possibilities, or those of some other substitute for the published bibliography originally contemplated.

For the purposes of this manual, however, it is assumed that a report favorable to the project is made by the bibliographer and that it is approved by the conference. In this case the agenda as provided in the report are worked over and annotated so as to form a permanent record of decisions made. Particular emphasis should be placed on the preparation and preservation of the document that results, since without it the expensive preliminary study of the project may be wasted or left in such a nebulous state that the value of the work already done is lost. With a clear record of actions in hand, however, the library has on file a justification for its decision that may be used to good advantage if the same subject is suggested again for bibliographical treatment. Another objective gained is that of eliminating the necessity of numerous later conferences to correct misunderstandings. And finally, as suggested in an earlier paragraph, in the event that it may become necessary to assign another bibliographer to the work, he can follow the pattern already set with a minimum of difficulty.

Notes of additional decisions reached during the conference are also added to the permanent record even if they are only tentative in character. They may include agreements suggested by the following topics:

1. Tentative decisions, now confirmed or changed, concerning the anticipated audience, costs, and limitations to be placed on personnel and time for the work leading to a published bibliography.

2. Specific scope.

3. Limitations to be placed on the sources to be searched, with the aim of making the bibliography selective rather than comprehensive, or vice versa.

4. Arrangement of entries: (a) alphabetical by author and title (main entry), subject, place, or authority responsible for the publication; (b) classified by subject; (c) chronological; (d) geographical; (e) by type of material; and (f) in various combinations of (a) through (e). (See also the discussion of Arrangement in the section of the manual devoted to Procedures.)

5. Inclusion of unusual miscellaneous details in entries, e.g., price, Library of Congress catalog card number, etc.

6. Purpose, extent, and style of annotations.

7. Provision of an index and its form, e.g., author, title, subject, special material, or a general index resulting from combinations of forms.

8. Publication.
   a. Method of reproducing the manuscript: by printing, photographing, multilithing, or other means.
   b. Number of copies in the edition.
   c. Method of distribution.

When decisions on the foregoing points have been made finally, or expressed in as close an estimate as possible, the conference has completed its work and has furnished to the bibliographer the means of drafting a succinct, formal statement concerning the project, which may be designated as a "work sheet."

D. The Work Sheet.

The work sheet is used in presenting to the authorities ultimately responsible for the publication a statement concerning salient points to be considered. It consists chiefly of a very much condensed version of information suggested above for inclusion in the bibliographer's report and covers the following points:

1. Proposed title of the publication.
2. Author (division and person).
3. Scope.
4. Need.
5. Estimated size, number of entries, format, and arrangement.
6. Estimated cost.
7. Estimated time for completion.
8. Size of the edition.
9. Administrative direction under which the work is to be done.
10. Editorial direction of the work.
11. Remarks.

When the work sheet has been approved by the proper authorities, it is forwarded to the Bibliography and Publications Committee for consideration. If the project receives administrative approval subsequent to affirmative recommendation by this committee, the bibliographer is instructed to go forward with plans already made and accepted. It is necessary, however, to provide for revisions of the original plans as these are required. A device known as a "progress report" may be used to achieve this aim.

E. The Progress Report.

Such reports are forwarded by the bibliographer to the supervisory official at stated intervals, possibly once a week. They serve as a statistical record of actual work accomplished, with respect to references examined, selected, described, edited, and annotated. Even more, they create for the bibliographer a convenient means for use in proposing solutions of new problems and revisions of earlier decisions as the progress of the work brings to light the desirability of such changes. Since these reports are susceptible to being annotated briefly and returned to the bibliographer for his guidance, they also enable his director to give supervision to the work of several bibliographers at once while keeping abreast also of other assignments, all with a minimum number of lengthy conferences.

II. PROCEDURES FOR PREPARING THE BIBLIOGRAPHY

The bibliographer who is assigned the duty of creating a guide to sources of information that other people can follow with profit does not proceed haphazardly. He accepts the fact that a substantial subject bibliography progresses safely through its various stages of development only if a reliable system is established for doing the work. First, the subject itself must be comprehended through the investigation of its literature. Items worthy of preliminary listing are tracked down through available sources, often by ingenious detective work. The unsifted list that results has to be evaluated, piece by piece, to eliminate marginal materials. The references that are retained require description in clear, consistent, and correct entries that result in ready identification of individual items. A scheme of orderly arrangement must be designed to place in serviceable relationships the individual works found worthy of inclusion. Finally, patient editorial revision, cooperation with the copyist, and proofreading are necessary to eliminate mistakes. The foregoing procedures comprise the subject matter of the pages that follow.

A. Investigation of the Literature.

The preparation of a scholarly bibliography requires not only a knowledge of general techniques but, even more, of the method to be used for mastering the bibliography of the subject, following orientation in its literature. This first aspect of procedures is considered in three divisions: (1) study of the subject; (2) selection of sources; and (3) location and selection of subject headings and names of authorities.

1. Study of the Subject. If the bibliographer is already thoroughly familiar with the subject of his assignment, his task is greatly simplified; if not, he must fall back upon the methodology of documentation in which he does have competence. Using that, he is able to move about between the card catalog, encyclopedias, dictionaries, handbooks, manuals, guides to reference books, and the like, to gain perspective of the work to come. During this phase of his study his aims are as follows: (a) to formulate a working definition of the subject; (b) to assess its more important subdivisions; (c) to acquire understanding of its vocabulary; (d) to gain a correct perspective of its history; (e) to investigate trends of research in the area of knowledge to which the subject belongs; and (f) to become acquainted with a few standard treatises on it if these exist.

The most significant publications that comprise the first fruits of his study he segregates, if that is possible, in a small reference collection which he uses again and again, and from which he draws a number of leads to additional materials. Always he pays attention to footnotes, references, and bibliographies that usually constitute substantial parts of such scholarly publications. Having, in the course of his study, drawn up a tentative outline of the obvious subdivisions of the subject under investigation, and committed it to writing, he is prepared to select the sources that are to be searched for the bibliographical coverage it seems wise to provide.

2. Selection of the Sources. The relative value of the sources and the order in which they should be consulted depend upon the nature of the individual project. However logical have been the order of procedures and the system with which they have been followed, circumstances individual to each separate compilation pose problems that are solved only by the aid of intelligence and imagination applied to the selection of bibliographical tools to be used. Under these circumstances it is a wise precaution to prepare a preliminary list of sources that promise to be useful. From such a list a record results that may be refined or enlarged as the work progresses, and also kept flexible by means of a separate entry for each source. During the course of the selection of sources, notes are added to the cards containing the entries, to indicate value or lack of it, and to give the limits of the search in terms of dates, volumes, and other general characteristics. In the case of sources that come out in serial form, it is particularly important to give the dates of issues examined.

A file of this kind on the bibliographer's desk has uses enough to justify the labor of maintaining it. By it his memory is refreshed, a possible successor in the project is guided and saved from repeating work already done, the systematic exploration of the subject is assured, and at last it results in an actual record of ground covered in searching. In some cases it may be highly desirable to incorporate the list with the preliminary matter in the published bibliography for the information of others who wish also to work in the area without retracing the steps of a predecessor. Types of sources of bibliographical information consulted are suggested under I and II below.

I. Unpublished Sources

Library catalogs:
- General
- Special collections
- Union catalogs
- Records of serial holdings

Shelflists:
- General libraries
- Special libraries

Divisional and personal records:
- Vertical files
- Unpublished bibliographies
- Personal records of reading and research

Individual and institutional authorities

In evaluating these unpublished sources, it may be said that the card catalog of an individual library provides the extensive bibliographical machinery without which all but the most obvious sources would be practically lost on the shelves. Union catalogs, on the other hand, describe and locate important publications in libraries from which they may be borrowed for examination, or to which readers may be referred for their use.

In the Library of Congress, bibliographers have access to the public Main Catalog, supplemented by nearly 15,000 reference works on open shelves; but this by no means exhausts the apparatus for bibliographical work provided by catalogs. In close physical proximity to the Main Catalog is the National Union Catalog containing more than 12,000,000 cards that describe reference and research materials found in some 700 cooperating libraries. Additional important sources of bibliographical information are: the Official Catalog, maintained in connection with cataloging operations; the Serial Record of bound and unbound serial publications in the Library of Congress; and the Process Information File of preliminary entries for works in process of final cataloging. A number of auxiliary catalogs also must be kept in mind when the languages, literatures, and subjects to which they relate are being investigated. Typical of such catalogs are those in the Manuscripts, Map, Music, and Orientalia Divisions. Catalogs in the Copyright Office, the Law Library, the Rare Books Division, the Microfilm Reading Room, the Division for the Blind, and the Slavic Room provide special facilities for the use of investigators in the several areas of interest represented by these sections of the Library. The foregoing examples illustrate but do not list the whole number of catalogs to which the bibliographer has access in the Library and about which he must endeavor to be well informed.

The shelflist, another unpublished source, in many American libraries is the closest approximation to a classified catalog that is obtainable. While it lacks most of the analytical entries of the true classified catalog, it nevertheless brings into orderly sequence records of publications related by subject -- records that may be widely separated by the alphabetical arrangement of a dictionary catalog. It also provides a guide to the arrangement of books on the shelves and thus serves as a stimulus to productive browsing, a practice that leads to some of the bibliographer's best finds. For a special collection developed to serve related interests, the shelflist is already a subject bibliography susceptible to expansion or contraction at need.

Less formal unpublished sources having bibliographical value accrue as divisions and individuals perform their functions in libraries. In that process they accumulate personal card files and unpublished bibliographies in which are recorded the results of their reading and reference work. Uncataloged ephemera, often difficult to find and frequently valuable, may be located in the divisional vertical files where alert members of the library staff have placed them.

Unpublished sources, even in the largest libraries of the world, are frequently less inclusive for a given subject than the special indexes, catalogs, abstracting journals, and miscellaneous published reference works that are part of a library's collections. Typical categories of these sources are the following:

II. Published Sources

Bibliographies

- Bibliographies of bibliographies

- National and trade
- Subject
- Public documents
- Dissertations
- "Research in progress"

Indexes
- Book reviews
- Essays
- Pamphlets
- Periodicals
- Subjects

Printed catalogs
- Documents
- General libraries
- National libraries
- Special libraries
- Special collections
- Subjects

Guides to literature
- General reference works
- Subjects
- Types, e.g., government publications

Abstracting services
- Subjects
- Form, e.g., dissertations

Miscellaneous sources
- Comprehensive works, e.g., encyclopedias and dictionaries
- Handbooks, manuals, etc.
- Lists of subject headings
- Monographic publications by authorities
- Monumental sets
- Periodicals featuring current book reviews, bibliographies, and announcements
- Periodicals not covered by indexing services
- Publications of associations, learned societies, special libraries, universities, etc.
- Standard texts

Publications in the foregoing categories are the tools of a bibliographer's trade and for the most part are described in his desk copies of the various guides to reference books. They are emphasized here, however, as a reminder of the necessity of making a systematic review of possible aids to bibliographical research each time a new problem is attacked. A caution may be in order also against overlooking some of the less obvious sources. In the field of dissertation bibliography, for instance, it is important to remember the annual lists of research in progress published in such journals as The American Economic Review, The American Political Science Review, The Professional Geographer, and Publications of the Modern Language Association of America. Again, while the great catalogs of government documents are well known, lists issued by bureaus, divisions, and departments may be less readily located and identified.[1/] Although retrospective bibliographies of bibliographies are a first line of defense against the disaster of repeating work already done, necessarily these compilations are out of date before they are completed; hence the bibliographies, book reviews, and news notes in journals appearing currently cannot be overlooked. The cumulative volumes of national and trade bibliographies are invaluable records of what is known about the output of printing in the world, country by country and period by period; but until the most recent number of the serial continuations of such bibliographies has been examined the bibliographer's estimate of complete coverage may be premature. Moreover, his examination, however faithfully carried out, will not produce satisfactory results unless he has familiarized himself with the terminology of the subject headings adopted by the compiler.

3. Location and Selection of Subject Headings and Names. One of the most helpful guides to terminology is Subject Headings Used in the Dictionary Catalogs of the Library of Congress, 5th edition (1948). This publication and its supplements are the sources from which to extract and list the headings and cross references that will lead the searcher through the unavoidable intricacies of so extensive a catalog. An introduction to "the rationale and basic rules of practice in the choice and use of subject headings," particularly in the Library of Congress, may be found in the Library's Subject Headings; a Practical Guide, by David J. Haykin (1951). Guidance to subject headings developed for some 29 special subject fields is provided in a "Bibliography of Subject Headings Lists, 1938-1952," a compilation found in the Journal of Cataloging and Classification (v. 8, Dec. 1952: 159-170), an official publication of the Division of Cataloging and Classification of the American Library Association.

It must be borne in mind, however, that subject headings used throughout large card catalogs cannot reflect constantly changing fashions in the use of terms, unless the wisdom of a Solomon and the purse of a Croesus are simultaneously available. For new terminology not yet firmly established or old terminology in process of change, the bibliographer must consult such sources as the indexing and abstracting publications in which the editors can afford to use headings that are more recent, expendable, and flexible. The same may be said of tables of contents and indexes in books. The necessary relationships must be made, therefore, between these various headings under which identical subjects may be listed, by means of the bibliographer's

---

[1/] "Problems of document bibliography: a symposium." College and research libraries, v. 15, Jan. 1954: 33-45. Z671.C6, v. 15

own addition to his file of pertinent cross references. Particularly when working on an extensive or complex bibliography, he will find it economical in the long view to prepare from the foregoing sources his own list of significant headings and cross references, a list enlarged as the use of the card catalog leads to the discovery of new headings through the tracing on the catalog cards.

This file, with individual entries on 3 x 5 cards arranged in alphabetical order, serves many purposes. It constitutes one of the records that give continuity to the work when new bibliographers are associated with the project. If annotations and an index are to be supplied, the list may be consulted as an aid to achieving preciseness and consistency of language in these two important elements of the bibliography. Most important of all, the file makes possible systematic searching for materials and at the same time protects the searcher from the forgetfulness and aberrations to which the "thinking machine" is prone, however earnest may be the effort to be precise.

Names of subjects are not the only desirable entries for this file. It is a satisfactory location also for names of persons and institutions engaged in furthering work in the field to which the bibliography is related. Such names tend to reappear as the investigation proceeds and when located in the proper reference works (such as biographical dictionaries and descriptive lists of institutions) frequently provide additional clues worth following.

B. Search for Materials.

The bibliographer now undertakes the solution of his next problem: the identification, location, and brief description of items to be examined and evaluated before they are selected for final inclusion in the bibliography. Forearmed for this attack by the background gained from study of the subject, by a list of promising subject headings and names to guide him, he proceeds to search out in much greater detail the materials described in the unpublished and published sources he has decided to use.

The two types of sources may be searched independently or interchangeably according to the requirements of the individual bibliography. The checking of sources is also interrupted, from time to time, by the examination of particularly significant works discovered during the search. In general, however, the aim is to make a fairly complete list of potentially desirable works before becoming too deeply involved in the final process of appraisal. Of course it is quite true that additional items come to light and are selected even at the eleventh hour, so that no dogmatic rule can be made concerning these procedures.

Bibliographers on the staff of the Library of Congress are relieved of the task of copying the printed cards that describe the items provisionally selected, because they may draw copies of the cards from the Card Division of the Library, using a simple form provided for the purpose. The form is used also to verify the Library of Congress card when it is received or to identify the item if its card is out of print.

Citations consisting of references to periodical articles, documents, separate monographs published in series, or other publications not described or analyzed in card catalogs require independent description by the bibliographer. Entries for these are derived from sources in which they are found, notably from periodical indexes, abstracting journals, and other published sources.

Time and energy spent in this clerical activity of copying constitute one of the most frustrating experiences in bibliographical work. But until copying as a part of searching is successfully mechanized, or until requisite clerical assistance can be afforded the bibliographer, careful transcription is unavoidable. Entries must be copied in sufficient detail to be both intelligible and consistent in form with the style followed throughout the bibliography. The temptation is ever present to use the highly condensed form of the data supplied in the typical index entry, without taking time, for example, to turn back to the list of titles indexed, and from that to supply the full title, as well as the place of publication if the latter is required for identification of a journal. Statements concerning volumes, pages, and dates rarely constitute a problem in copying, since without most of these details the reference would be meaningless; but the order and wording of these may require change. Abbreviations of corporate names and of words that describe special features may appear; these also must be clarified if a key to abbreviations appears in the source consulted. Errors in copying must be caught by faithful proofreading.

A symbol added to the entry to show the source from which it came may be useful in connection with a long, complex bibliography, particularly for the convenience of an editor who may wish to question something in the reference. Data not supplied in the source are secured and added by the bibliographer, e. g., call number and Library of Congress card number.

During the phase of the work devoted to searching, the bibliographer deliberately errs on the side of inclusiveness, to avoid retracing his steps later. But even in this stage he employs all of the criteria of selection that may be used with safety. By keeping constantly in mind decisions concerning scope, etc., made during the period of planning, he is able to achieve a considerable amount of screening even before examination. The collection of a forest of references to unimportant or irrelevant materials merely for the sake of numerical completeness is a deterrent rather than an aid to bibliographical excellence.

No rule can be given as to when the period of search should be considered satisfactorily concluded, for the bibliographer is carried on from one reference to another by new leads as these appear. One fairly reliable evidence that the saturation point has been reached, however, is apparent when identical items are found at the end of every path that is followed.

As soon as the decision to stop all but supplementary searching has been reached, the entries collected are filed in the order most convenient for consultation, usually alphabetically by author, and by title when the main entry is under title. The bibliography is now in preliminary form, ready for revision when the references have been examined and evaluated.

C. Evaluation of References.

The familiar canons of book selection are followed in choosing references that are to be cited in the bibliography. These include among others: (a) authority of the author; (b) scope, purpose, and style of the work; (c) limitations in appeal because of language, dates, and unusual attainments requisite to successful use; and (d) special features, e.g., bibliographies, footnotes, maps, indexes, etc. Importance of references not available for examination may be deduced also from citations in authoritative treatises, book reviews, bibliographies, and other sources. Clearly this is one of the most critical stages of the bibliographer's work. If his selection is good, he is on his way to creating a safe guide for use in exploring a body of material and in increasing knowledge of a subject. On the other hand, if his work has been impressionistic, superficial, or hasty rather than rapid, the result is inadequate and very probably misleading.

If the bibliography is to be annotated and indexed, problems incident to those undertakings should be faced at the time of evaluation and before the references are returned to the shelves. Brief notes may be attached to entries indicating the reasons for inclusion, special features, and terminology best adapted for later use in annotating and indexing; but complete annotations are not usually written until the bibliography has been finally arranged. At that time new relationships become apparent, the relative significance of each work may be more justly appraised, and redundant statements eliminated. Repetitions of identical facts and monotony of style also are more easily avoided if all important annotations of a specific bibliography are written consecutively.

D. Preparation of Entries.

As each piece passes through the bibliographer's hands for evaluation, it is compared with the provisional entry already established for it. If this entry is in the form of a printed catalog card, its series number, call number, author or title heading, and the elements of the entry are already supplied. These are verified and additions that are indicated by the purpose of the bibliography are made, as, for example, a note to point up the presence of a special feature significant for the bibliography but too detailed for inclusion when the publication was cataloged.

Entries in manuscript, collected and prepared by the bibliographer, require careful revision. Not only the accuracy of the information provided but also the legibility with which it is recorded are checked, so that no slurring of letters or unintelligible abbreviations will remain to vex the bibliographer when he gives the work final revision after entries have been arranged according to the plan adopted.

E. Arrangement of Entries.

A plan of logical arrangement frequently develops from the bibliographer's knowledge of the subject, gained not only from an initial study but also from all the procedures of selecting, evaluating, and describing materials. Such an arrangement is tested, of course, by comparison with that of other bibliographies which reflect the preferences of specialists in the field. In the Library of Congress the established classification schedules of the institution are useful in a similar way. In the last analysis, however, it is his individual responsibility to think through the problems of arrangement posed by his individual bibliography and to solve them. Fortunately, numerous plans of adaptations and permutations are open for selection in the arrangement of entries. Among the schemes of arrangement most commonly used are those that derive from the alphabet, those that are based on classification by subjects, and those that separate materials into categories by type of publication.

1. Alphabetical Arrangement. The simplest plan of arrangement is the one based on the alphabet. Through its use a variety of emphases may be given, according to the nature of the elements selected as the basis of the arrangement, e. g., author, title, place, subject, or sponsoring institution.

a. By Author's Name. Arrangement by author is usually chosen when the names of the persons and corporate bodies responsible for the intellectual content of the works to be included provide the most significant and direct approach to identification and location of the items. Under the name of author, titles may be arranged alphabetically for ease in locating specific items. Chronological arrangement by date of publication may be preferred when it is important to show the progress of the writer's work or the timeliness of his contributions to a developing subject. When the authors represent obvious and important relationships on the basis of language, nationality, or some other common factors, entries may be grouped by these relationships before the alphabetical list within each group begins. This combination of arrangements may be particularly useful in the case of a long bibliography.

b. By Title of Publication. A bibliography of serials that have main entries under titles is ordinarily arranged alphabetically by title; for an extensive list, however, division by region or subject may precede the alphabetical arrangement.

c. By Place of Publication. A bibliography of newspapers or local imprints may be arranged alphabetically by place of publication. Here again a prior general regional breakdown may precede the alphabetical listing of specific localities.

d. By Subject. A bibliography arranged alphabetically by subject headings presents certain difficulties. Among these is the necessity for frequent cross references or multiple entries for the same item. The alphabetical subject arrangement may be appropriate, however, in cases of rapidly developing fields not susceptible to systematic subdivision, or when all the headings relate to a relatively limited field.

e. By Sponsoring Institution. When neither the personal author nor the title of the publication ranks in importance with the sponsoring agency, the agency legitimately may form the basis of arrangement. Under its name the various publications it has sponsored are then arranged by the scheme most useful for accomplishing the purpose of the bibliography.

2. Classified Arrangement. A common form of arrangement employed by bibliographers for an extensive compilation is that of the classified list, arranged on the basis of a systematic division or analysis of the subject of the bibliography. Author, title, or other kinds of arrangement are employed in such lists under each subdivision.

There are, however, several difficulties connected with the preparation of classified lists which should be borne in mind by the bibliographer. It is not always easy to make a systematic division of a given subject, and even if the theoretical division is accomplished, the material to be arranged does not always fit the scheme. A theoretical scheme may be too detailed or too general to accommodate the material.

These difficulties can most often be overcome if the bibliographer experiments with variant schemes and a sample selection of titles before determining the final form of classification to be used.

An index which provides appropriate cross references and serves as a guide to authors, and to titles as main entries, is a practical necessity in all but brief and simple bibliographies.

3. Chronological Arrangement. A bibliography may be arranged chronologically, either in terms of the chronology and development of its subject or in terms of the publication dates of the items to be arranged. The former type is suitable only for bibliographies of a subject which has had a long history and presents the possibility of division into significant epochs. The latter type may be suitable for some subjects as, for example, the bibliography of an individual author, of local imprints, of the development of a specific category of literature, etc.

4. Regional Arrangement. The notion of region, like that of chronology, has a double significance for the bibliographer, referring either to the subject or to the place of publication of an entry. In both senses regional divisions may function as either major or minor categories in a bibliography. The present and increasing interest in area studies presents to the bibliographer the problems of integrating regional with subject and chronological divisions. The bibliographer should be aware that, unlike dates, the names of regions and their accepted boundaries are constantly changing and even disappearing. Nevertheless, an increasing volume of literature on regions and areas is likely to appear and the bibliographer will find in regional breakdowns a valuable aid in the organization of materials.

5. Arrangement by Type of Material. When the subject of a bibliography is limited, but the types of materials to which reference is made are numerous, it is sometimes convenient to use type as the basis of arrangement. Monographic works, periodicals, newspapers, manuscripts, microfilms, and public documents are thought of as types in this connection. The result of this kind of arrangement is that of showing at a glance blocks of materials in which the subject is treated, but ordinarily it is not a plan to be recommended except in combination with other schemes.

When entries have been arranged according to a scheme or combination of schemes selected by the bibliographer, he reviews the results of the organization that has been achieved. At once it may become apparent that certain subdivisions of the subject are inadequately covered. On the other hand, subdivisions that are swollen with references may require further subdivision. Still others may be represented by such substantial individual works that publications of more limited utility become unnecessary and may be eliminated from the bibliography. In some cases individual works in different subdivisions overlap one another in subject content to such an extent that a new analysis may be required. For all of these reasons the advice of specialists, or of the instigators of the project, may profitably be taken at this point, as well as that of authorities in the library who are ultimately responsible for the completed product.

After the resulting conferences have been held and such adjustments made as may be necessary, the question of writing annotations is faced. For considerations that govern this part of the work and for suggestions concerning the style to be used, the bibliographer is referred to Appendix C in which Annotations are discussed. Arrangement and the preparation of annotations should be completed before entries and their annotations receive final editorial revision by the bibliographer.

F. Editorial Revision of Entries.

Inevitably entries established from published sources, as well as from card catalogs, represent variations in style that must be eliminated by exceedingly careful editorial revision. Rules for cataloging change over the years, not to mention the inevitable inconsistencies in the application of rules. As a result, differences are reflected in the printed cards. Style manuals of firms responsible for published works from which references have been copied also specify different procedures. In the process of drawing references from such sources, the bibliographer naturally eliminates many of the stylistic variations that he encounters. Now at last, however, he must assume responsibility for bringing all entries into consistent bibliographical form and for eliminating from them typographical and other errors.

In the Library of Congress the style recommended for general bibliographical work, exclusive of that in such special fields as law, music, rare books, etc., is described and illustrated in the section of this manual entitled "Bibliographical Style." The Index provides a convenient guide to the use of the rules given there, and examples of printed catalog cards with editorial markings are shown in Appendix B on Use of Printed Catalog Cards. The bibliographer is warned, however, that no manual can or should provide for every contingency. In the absence of specific rules that are applicable to his material and consistent with the purpose of the bibliography, it is his responsibility to follow principles expressed in the manual, while establishing new forms as these may be necessary.

The procedure of editing bibliographical entries presents problems quite different from those faced in editing textual matter. In a text, associations of words in sentences and sentences in paragraphs carry the understanding as well as the eye forward and expedite the discovery of inconsistencies and errors. Editorial revision of entries in a bibliography, on the other hand, not only calls for familiarity with rules of entry and the ability to detect violations, but also requires skill in discovering mistakes in details that are so familiar as to be difficult to scan objectively. The latter situation exists particularly with reference to fullness of names, punctuation, abbreviations, the form of the imprint, and the deletion of parts of the descriptive detail on printed cards that are not to be used, e. g., statement of size, subject tracings, superfluous notes, etc.

Another prime necessity in this type of editing must be reiterated at this point; namely, that of making any handwritten entries, if their use is unavoidable, completely understandable to the copyist who will transcribe the bibliography before it is published. Indention, spacing, and the whole stylized organization of the elements of the entry are the responsibility of the bibliographer, not of the copyist. Idiosyncrasies of handwriting, however unimportant, are frequently confusing when a copyist is not familiar with them and unless eradicated may cause mistakes or such frequent conferences as to be prohibitive in terms of the time required.

When the file of entries has had complete editorial revision by the compiler, the corrected bibliography is ready to be submitted for final approval. Since progress reports and conferences incident to them have kept the supervising authority and the bibliographer in close touch throughout work on the project, no drastic change need be expected at this point. However, if the institution maintains an editorial review board to pass on its publications, a representative of the latter group is also invited to examine the manuscript and to suggest whatever further editorial revision he may consider desirable.

G. Instructions for the Copyist.

Whether the bibliography as finally approved is to be printed, photographed, or reproduced by some other process, a fair copy of it must be prepared in page form from the bibliographer's file of annotated cards. This step necessitates a thorough briefing of the copyist on variations and details that may prove puzzling. A preliminary table of contents is prepared by the bibliographer as a guide to the placing of headings and their subdivisions. The width of margins, not only in relation to readability and appearance but also with reference to the style of binding, is indicated. If the bibliography is to be indexed the copyist is expected to assign a consecutive number to each item and must be informed of this necessity. Finally, if editorial markings are unusual or unfamiliar, these must be explained.

H. Reading the Copy.

It is the responsibility of the copyist to submit a carbon copy of the original that has been prepared for reproduction. Two purposes are served by this copy: (1) corrections that result from proofreading may be made on it without defacing the fair copy; and (2) the bibliographer is able to use it for marking in preparation for indexing. The proofreader's marks given in the Style Manual of the United States

Government Printing Office (1953), p. 2, are those followed in the Library of Congress. If the bibliography is printed, it must be proofread again in galley proof.

PART TWO

BIBLIOGRAPHICAL STYLE

SOURCES AND SYMBOLS

Published sources consistently used to establish standards of bibliographical style are given below. The code letters by which successive references to these publications are made appear in the column on the left. Occasional references to additional sources are provided in the bibliography of style manuals and other works which appears as Appendix F or in footnotes.

Symbols	Chief Sources
ALA	American Library Association. Division of Cataloging and Classification. A. L. A. cataloging rules for author and title entries. 2d ed., edited by Clara Beetle. Chicago, American Library Association, 1949. 265 p. Z695.A52 1949
RDC	U. S. Library of Congress. Descriptive Cataloging Division. Rules for descriptive cataloging in the Library of Congress. Washington, 1949. 141 p. Z695.U4735 1949 ----- ----- Supplement. 1949-51. Washington, 1952. 19 p. Z695.U4735 1949 Suppl.

Additional Sources

GPO	U. S. Government Printing Office. Style manual. Rev. ed. Washington, 1953. 492 p. Z253.U58 1953
CS	U. S. Library of Congress. Processing Dept. Cataloging service. Bulletin 1- June 1945- Washington. Z695.U437 Established "as a medium of occasional communication" of information concerning cataloging activities in the Library of Congress, this bulletin from time to time includes statements of additions to cataloging rules and changes in them.

I. BOOKS, PAMPHLETS, AND OTHER MONOGRAPHIC PUBLICATIONS

Outline

I. BOOKS, PAMPHLETS, AND OTHER MONOGRAPHIC PUBLICATIONS

I. The entry. Each entry in a bibliography includes a record of information contained in a variety of elements, designed to identify the reference in libraries or for purchase, and to indicate its significance in relation to the purpose of the compilation.

A. Elements and their arrangement. Elements in such an entry describe as many details as are justified by the composition of the individual work for which entry is being made. These elements are arranged in the sequence indicated below.

> Author heading, title, subtitle or alternate title, author statement in certain instances, edition statement, imprint, collation, series note, call number or location symbol. Supplementary notes are added, if necessary, to supply additional information. Each note usually constitutes a separate paragraph unless several notes bear on one point and therefore may be combined in the same paragraph. An annotation follows when the item warrants that additional comment and constitutes the last paragraph of the whole entry.

B. Punctuation. The insertion of punctuation marks in and between elements of a simple bibliographical description is illustrated in the following example.

> Johnson, John W. Writing research papers; a guide for students. 2d ed., rev. Washington, Eldman and Jones, 1952. 201 p. (College manuals, no. 2)
> PE1478.J56

More complicated descriptions require additional punctuation. Generally in the body of the entry an ellipsis (three dots) is used to indicate the abridgement of a long title; brackets are placed around elements or parts of elements supplied by the bibliographer; and double punctuation is avoided by omitting final periods and commas after brackets, ellipses, and parentheses. However, the bibliographer may be guided by his own judgment concerning the use of these punctuation marks in the body of the entry.

The plus sign is substituted for the dash used by catalogers to indicate an open entry, which implies the later provision of additional information; no period is used after the plus sign. Question marks follow details about which uncertainty exists, as in the case of a missing or incomplete date requiring an approximation. No punctuation follows the call number proper or location symbol.

Ceylon journal of science. Section G. Anthropology. v. 1+ July 2, 1924+ Colombo. irregular.
GN1. C56

Conklin, George W., comp. Handy manual of useful information and world's atlas for mechanics, merchants, editors, lawyers ... also a compilation of facts on 2,000 subjects. Rev. and corr. ed. Chicago, Laird and Lee, c1889. 440 p. AG105. C7 1889

Marggraf, Karl A. Zur Rassenmorphologie des äusseren Ohres. [Berlin-Dahlem, Ahnenerbe-Stiftung Verlag, 1939?] [349]-393 p. illus., diagrs.
QM507. M33

Inaug.-Diss.--Tübingen.
"Mitteilungen der Anthropologischen Gesellschaft in Wien, 1939, LXIX. Band, S. 349-393."
Bibliography: p. 392-393.

C. Capitalization.

1. In English.

a. Words and expressions. (ALA, p. 239-240; GPO, p. 17-50)

Proper names and their derivatives.
Common nouns and adjectives that are parts of proper names.
Names of organized bodies.
Names of countries and administrative divisions.
Names of regions, localities, and geographic divisions.
Names of calendar divisions.
Names of historic events.
Religious terms including names applied to the Deity, to the Bible and versions of it, other sacred writings, confessions of faith, and religious bodies and their adherents.
Titles that precede names of persons.
Titles that follow names of persons, in the case of a head or assistant head of a state or governmental unit, a member of a diplomatic corps, a ruler, prince, queen, or princess.
Titles in religion that indicate high office, such as Bishop and Archbishop, and pronouns, adjectives, and common nouns in religious names, e.g., Father Raphael of Our Lady of Perpetual Help.

Names and epithets of peoples, races, and tribes.

b. Titles.

(1) Monographs and articles.

(a) In entries. The first word is capitalized in the titles of publications, papers, documents, newspapers, acts, laws, articles, chapters in books, etc. Other words in the title are not capitalized except as described in the preceding paragraph. (See also RDC, Appendix II, Capitalization, p. 111.) This rule applies to the capitalization of a title quoted in the body of an entry, to an alternative title introduced by "or" or its equivalent, and to titles referred to in supplementary notes and footnotes. If a title, other than that of an anonymous work, is the main entry for a publication and it begins with an article, the word following the article is also capitalized.

This style of capitalization has been adopted for the following reasons: economy in editorial revision of Library of Congress printed catalog cards; readability; and consistency of entries that are not included in textual matter.

Titles of separate publications quoted in the body of the entry and in supplementary notes (except formalized "contents" notes) are italicized (or underscored), and titles of articles, chapters in books, etc., are enclosed in quotation marks.

(b) In textual matter. The first word and all important words are capitalized in the titles cited in textual matter, i.e., forewords, prefaces, introductions and explanatory matter in essay form. These titles are also italicized or enclosed in quotation marks, whichever is applicable.

(c) In annotations. If the annotations in a bibliography are predominantly of the character of reviews, digests, or abstracts, the rule for capitalizing titles cited in textual matter is followed throughout the bibliography. However, if the majority of the annotations are brief, titles are capitalized according to the rule for titles in entries.

(d) In indexes. Titles of publications listed in the index to a bibliography are capitalized and italicized, or enclosed in quotation marks, in compliance with the rule for citing titles in textual matter.

(2) Series. Only the first word and words described under Words and Expressions are capitalized in titles of series in the body of the entry, in notes, or in annotations. They are neither italicized nor placed in quotation marks.

c. Imprints. The first word and all important words in the publisher statement are capitalized.

2. In foreign languages, capitalization of words, expressions, names, titles of persons, titles of publications, etc., is provided in accordance with practices acceptable to the country whose language is being used. Guidance for capitalization in foreign languages is found in the following sources:

RDC, Appendix II, p. 111-120, and Supplement 1949-51, p. 3-4.
GPO, sections on capitalization in "Foreign Languages," p. 329-426.
CS, no. 25, Dec. 1951: 3-4.

U. S. Government Printing Office. Manual of foreign languages for the use of librarians, bibliographers ... and printers. 4th ed., rev. and enl. by Georg F. von Ostermann. New York, Central Book Co., 1952. 414 p. Z253.U581 1952

Rules for capitalization in English are followed in the case of languages for which no rules have been included in the publications cited above.

3. Collation. "Each item in the collation statement of illustrative matter is lower-cased," e.g., illus., diagr., port.

D. Indention. The importance of the heading under which the entry appears is emphasized, and aid in locating a specific entry under its heading is provided, by the use of hanging indention. This is a form of indention in which the heading is extended a designated number of spaces to the left of the block in which the body of the entry is set. Notes and annotations are arranged in paragraph form, using a similar indention inward from the line fixed by the main part of the entry.

Hymes, James L. A healthy personality for your child. Washington, U. S. Govt. Print. Off., 1952. 23 p. illus. (U. S. Children's Bureau. Publication, no. 337) HQ769. H975

This pamphlet is a popular version of part of "A healthy personality for every child," a digest of the fact-finding Report submitted to the Mid-century White House Conference on Children and Youth.

Inter-American affairs; an annual survey. no. 1-5; 1941-45. New York, Columbia University Press. 5 v. F1418. I592

A. P. Whitaker, editor.

II. Author and title entries.

A. Author entry.

1. Definition of author. "The author is considered to be the person or body chiefly responsible for the intellectual content of the book ... the maker of the work or the person or body immediately responsible for its existence. Thus, a person who collects and puts together the writings of several authors (compiler or editor) may be said to be the author of a collection. A corporate body may be considered the author of publications issued in its name or by its authority." (ALA, p. 3, 230)

2. Rules of entry. The basic principles governing author entry are expressed in rules provided in ALA. The forms in which these rules are applied by bibliographers in certain cases vary from those suggested in ALA. Factors influencing such adaptations are: the physical form in which bibliographies are issued, with numerous items recorded on one page rather than one item to an entry, as in a card catalog; the distribution of published bibliographies to a scattered clientele to whom entries must be self-explanatory; and the expendable character of a bibliography in comparison to the permanence of a card catalog. Procedures to be followed in these exceptional cases are described in the following pages, in which explanations of recurring bibliographical problems are also offered. Such explanations are documented by frequent references to pertinent sections of ALA and RDC.

3. Personal author.

   a. Fullness of name. Works by an individual author are normally entered under his surname, followed by his first name and middle initial or initials. If, however, he is more readily identified by another form of the name, such as the one that appears habitually on the title pages of his books, that form is preferred.

Dickson, William E. R.
Read, Herbert E.
 but
Bennett, Arnold, not Bennett, Enoch A.
Shaw, George Bernard, not Shaw, George B.
Wilson, Woodrow, not Wilson, Thomas W.

Efforts to discover the first name of an author, if an initial only is known, are limited to search in the catalogs of the Library of Congress and examination of the usual biographical reference books, except in an unusual case, such as that of confusion in the identity of two or more persons.

b. Dates. Dates of birth and death are omitted from the author heading for personal names. If, however, the date of the author's birth is an aid to an identification that is otherwise obscure, it is added, e. g., Johnson, Maxwell W., b. 1888; Johnson, Maxwell W., b. 1917. This is a case in which the designation "Jr." does not apply.

c. Titles of nobility, office, address, etc. (ALA, 41, p. 87-88; 50-57, p. 97-109)

(1) Titles included. Titles of nobility, higher offices or ranks, and courtesy are included in italics, usually with the full names of persons, in the author heading, in the form shown below.

Manning, William Thomas, Bp.
Spellman, Francis Joseph, Cardinal.
Montgomery, Bernard Law Montgomery,
 1st viscount.
Wentworth, Judith Blunt-Lytton, baroness.
Pope-Hennessy, Dame Una.
Walpole, Sir Hugh.
Reventlow, Joseph Karl, Graf zu.
Sforza, Carl, conte.

(2) Titles omitted. Titles usually omitted from the author heading are those of: address (Herr, Mrs., etc.); minor ecclesiastical and governmental titles (reverend, governor, etc.); titles of military and naval personnel (general, major, etc.); and academic and professional titles (professor, doctor, etc.). Such titles should be included, however, in cases in which their use aids in the distinction between similar names, or in the identification of obscure or incomplete names, e. g., Firman, Brother;

Maruelle, Captain; and Smith, Dr. William.

d. Anonymous works. If the name of the author of a work published anonymously has been discovered, the item is entered under the discovered name in brackets. A "see" reference in the index, if there is one, otherwise in the body of the bibliography, may be made from the title to the author's name. When the name of the author remains unknown, entry is under title.[1]

e. Pseudonymous works are entered under the author's name, supplied in brackets, when the name is known. The pseudonym is given in the author statement following the title.

> [Starkey, James] Essays and recollections, by Seumas O'Sullivan [pseud.]

Two exceptions are made to the foregoing rule: (1) the author desires that his name be withheld; and (2) the pseudonym is better known by well-informed people than the real name. In both cases entry is under the pseudonym.

In an index, a "see" reference is made from the pseudonym to the real name, or vice versa, as required. If no index is provided, the reference appears in the body of the bibliography.

> O'Sullivan, Seumas, pseud. See Starkey, James.

If both the real name and the pseudonym appear in the work, both are given in the author statement, e. g., "by Sagittarius (Olga Katzin)."

f. Married women. Normally, entry for a married woman is under her husband's surname, followed by her first name and maiden name in parentheses.

> Bacon, Harriet (Winser), not Bacon, Harriet W.

Exceptions to this rule are made as necessary, for instance under the following conditions:

(1) After her marriage the author continues to use her maiden name by which she is better known as a writer; she is therefore entered

---

[1] The term "Anonymous" or "Anon." is not used as the heading of such entries, since its employment would bring together an unrelated mass of miscellaneous material, thus increasing the difficulty of identification.

under the latter.

Furman, Bess, _not_ Armstrong, Bess (Furman)

(2) The author has resumed her maiden name after a divorce and prefers to be known under that.

Bird, Letitia, _not_ Blank, Letitia (Bird)

(3) The author has been married a second time but retains the surname of her first husband in her professional capacity as a writer.

Buck, Pearl (Sydenstricker), _not_ Walsh, Pearl (Sydenstricker)

In any case of doubt as to which form of the names readers may know best, a cross reference is provided for guidance, e. g., Fuller, Margaret. _See_ Ossoli, Sara Margaret (Fuller) _marchesa_ d'.

The title of address, _Mrs._, is not used in the author heading under which a married woman is entered unless the use of her husband's forename instead of her own makes it essential, e. g., Compton, _Mrs._ Charles.

g. _Variant forms of author's name._ When the form of an author's name found on the title page of a publication differs markedly from that selected for use in the heading, the former is repeated in the author statement.

Jovichić, Lenka A. The biography of a Serbian diplomat, by Lena A. Yovitchitch.

Important variants of personal names not selected for use in headings are entered with special care in the index as "see" references.

h. _Editor, compiler, translator._ When the relation of an editor, compiler, or translator to a publication is so formative that he may be considered immediately responsible for the existence of the work, his name constitutes the author heading. It is followed by the appropriate designation, e. g., ed., comp., tr. However, collections are usually entered under title (1) if the responsibility of the editor or editors seems to be slight, (2) if their names do not appear prominently in the publication, (3) if it is known that the work is generally referred to by title, and (4) if there are frequent changes of editor. The title entry is preferred for any serial publication because it is assumed that the editor will change.

Migne, Jacques P., ed. Patrologiae cursus completus. Paris, J. P. Migne, 1857-66.

Waley, Arthur, tr. Translations from the Chinese.

but

The Pageant of America, a pictorial history of the United States; Ralph H. Gabriel, editor.

Handbook of Latin American studies. no. [1]+ 1935+ Gainesville, Fla., University of Florida Press, 1936+ annual. Z1605.H23

The present editor (1954) is Francisco Aguilera. Formerly published by the Harvard University Press, Cambridge, Mass.

i. Joint authors. The names of two or three personal authors, collaborators, or contributors who are jointly responsible for a work are included in the author heading except when the heading is to be repeated in a "dash" form of entry.[2] They are entered in the order used on the title page of the publication; only the name of the first is inverted.

Cairns, Huntington, Allen Tate, and Mark Van Doren, eds. Invitation to learning. New York, Random House, 1941. 431 p. PN523.C3

If more than three authors are jointly responsible for the publication, the name of the first is entered as the author heading, followed by the expression "and others" in italics. At the discretion of the bibliographer, names omitted from the author heading are supplied in the author statement. Their names may then be indexed to meet the requirements of readers who know the book best under a name other than that of the first author. Names of secondary helpers and participants are omitted from the bibliographical entry.

Ordinarily names of joint authors, other than the first, are not recorded alphabetically in the body of the bibliography, either by duplicate entry or by cross references. The index entry is considered sufficient.

---

[2] In the latter case only the name of the first author is given in the heading.

Publications for which two or three corporate authors are jointly responsible are entered under an author heading consisting only of the name of the first corporate author mentioned on the title page. If the bibliographer wishes to include the names of additional corporate authors concerned, they may be given in the author statement or in a note or annotation.

The names of the second and the third joint authors are disregarded in alphabetizing entries under the first author's name. Arrangement is first by his name and secondarily by the title of the publication.

4. *Corporate author*. Works issued by the authority of governments, societies, institutions, and miscellaneous corporate bodies are entered under the name of the organization responsible for them. In many instances, such corporate bodies have subordinate units. When these are authors, their names constitute an essential subdivision of the main author entry. To indicate this relation, they are written in italics, e. g., Minnesota. University. *Graduate School.* *Social Science Research Center*.

a. *Abbreviation.* Corporate names are ordinarily written in full; e. g., Permanent Committee on Geographical Names for British Official Use; and Joint Committee on Materials for Research.

Geographical names at the beginning of corporate author headings with subheadings are abbreviated in only two cases: Great Britain (Gt. Brit.) and United States (U. S.). When names of states, territories, counties, provinces, etc., follow another geographical word they are abbreviated and written in italics, e. g., Salem, *Mass.*

The word Department (Dept.) is regularly abbreviated in a subsidiary section of a corporate author heading.

Alexandria, *Va.* *Dept. of Water and Sewage*.
Gt. Brit. *Home Dept.* *Water Gas Committee*.
Hampstead, *Eng.* *Borough Treasurer's Dept.*

b. *Types of corporate authors.*

(1) *Governments.* Rules of bibliographical style to be followed in establishing headings and providing entries for the publications of governments and their agencies are included in the section on Documents. It should be noted, however, that "certain classes of institutions and bodies, maintained, controlled or owned by governments and not mainly or exclusively performing routine administrative functions in a department or service, are ordinarily not to be entered under the name of governments as department subheadings ... that is, they are to be treated according to

the rules governing institutions and bodies," e.g., Reconstruction Finance Corporation, not U.S. Reconstruction Finance Corporation.[3] Rules of entry for the works of these organizations are provided in the sections on Societies and Institutions below. (See also ALA, 72A, Exception; p. 127.)

(2) Societies.[4] (ALA, 91-91C, p. 148-151; 93-101B, p. 154-165) For bibliographical purposes, societies may be defined as groups of persons organized for the accomplishment of certain common objectives. These may be social, political, ethical, professional, scientific, fraternal, benevolent, and other organizations. Typical societies, sometimes called academies, are those having a membership associated for the advancement of learning. The corporate entity of a society resides in its membership, usually widely distributed through a region, locality, or nation, and not necessarily in the place where its headquarters, it any, may be located.

The name of a society as stated in its works oonstitutes the preferred form of its corporate heading, provided the name leads to ready identification, e.g., Chicago Lumber Dealers Association. Works of international societies, having authorized names in various languages, are entered under the English form if given in the publications of the society; otherwise, under the form most commonly used.

Names of societies having a nation-wide membership tend to be sufficiently familiar for purposes of identification, even if their names lack such distinctive elements as designations of localities.

Academy of Motion Picture Arts and Sciences.
American Academy of Arts and Letters.
American Anthropological Association.
American Library Association.
Colonial Dames of America.
Gesellschaft Deutscher Metallhütten- und Bergleute.
National Association for the Advancement of Colored People.
Sociedad Nacional de Industrias.

---

[3] Childs, James B. Author entry for government publications. Washington, U.S. Govt. Print. Off., 1941. p. 3-4, 5. Z6951.G7C54 1941

[4] The initial article is retained in the heading of a society or institution only if necessary for clearness.

If there is doubt concerning the ease with which the society may be identified, its location is indicated in the author heading by adding at the end, following a comma, the italicized name of the place with which the society is associated. Four circumstances are thought particularly to justify such an addition: (a) the activities of the society take place in one locality; (b) the corporate name may be easily confused with a similar or identical name attached to a different society; (c) the society is located in a foreign country and its national affiliation may be expressed most simply by the addition of a place name; and (d) the headquarters of the society not having been ascertained, the name of a larger geographical unit, such as a country or a state, is supplied to facilitate identification. In the last case, parentheses are used around the geographical names.

French History Society, *New York.*
Laerde selskab, *Aarhus*, *Denmark.*
Polskie Towarzystwo Geologiczne, *Cracow.*
Sociedad de Artistas y Escritores Jóvenes (*Mexico*)

If a society signifies its incorporation by the use of a term such as "inc.," after its name, the abbreviation is omitted. If, however, the name begins with the word "incorporated" or if that word is an essential part of the name, it is retained. (For Religious Societies and Institutions see ALA, 115-130; p. 173-198.)

(3) *Institutions.* (ALA, 92-93C, p. 151-156; 94, p. 157-158; 102-102B, p. 166-167; 103-104, p. 167-168)

(a) Since an institution, unlike a society, performs its proper functions through the use of an establishment in a definite place, usually in a specific building or buildings, it is logical to use the place name as the entry word when assigning author headings for the works of institutions such as libraries, museums, churches, colleges, art galleries, hospitals, etc. This is particularly true when the actual corporate name begins with an indeterminate term, such as "public library," "university of," and "gallery of." Foreign institutions, exclusive of those in the British Empire, are also thought to be known best under place of location, even if their names are distinctive. In these corporate author headings under name of place, italics are not used except in subheadings.

Atlanta. Carnegie Library.
Buffalo. University.
Chicago. University.

Cleveland. Euclid Avenue Congregational Church.
Dresden. Gemälde-Galerie.
Florence. Galleria degli Uffizi.
Pittsburgh. Carnegie Library. Lawrenceville Branch.
Seville. Biblioteca Colombina.

(b) American institutions and those located in the British Empire, having names that begin with proper nouns or adjectives, are entered under these distinctive names. If, however, the initials of a personal name occur at the beginning of the corporate name, they are dropped and the surname only is used. If desired, the full name of a donor or the person honored in this way may be supplied in a note or annotation. The place of location of an institution is supplied after its name, however distinctive the form of the name may be, unless the reputation of the institution is such as to make the mention of its location superfluous. When location is in an obscure place, or in a place having a name identical with another place in a different location, the name of the appropriate larger geographical unit is added to the institutional name. (For Religious Societies and Institutions see ALA, 115-130; p. 173-198.)

Agnes Scott College, Decatur, Ga.
Isabella Stewart Gardner Museum, Boston.
Jafflinn Memorial Institute, New York, not J. F. Jafflinn, etc.
Lincoln Memorial University, Harrogate, Tenn.
Massachusetts Institute of Technology.
Peter Bent Brigham Hospital, Boston.
Pierpont Morgan Library, New York.
Walters Art Gallery, Baltimore.
Willamette University, Salem, Or.

(4) Miscellaneous bodies. (ALA, 131-149; p. 199-214)

(a) Diplomatic congresses and conferences. (ALA, 131; p. 199-200) Agreements and conventions and other publications resulting from the work of congresses and conferences called to promote international understanding through consultation, or to conduct meetings leading to the adoption of pacts and treaties, are entered under the name of the conference. The place of meeting is supplied, in italics, followed by the date, e.g., Diplomatic Conference for the Establishment of

International Conventions for the Protection of Victims of War, Geneva, 1949.

Conferences or congresses, including those for the dilopmatic negotiation of peace between belligerent powers, are entered under the individual name by which they are commonly known. If no individual name can be discovered, they are entered under the name of the place of meeting.

Conference for Conclusion and Signature of Treaty of Peace with Japan, San Francisco, 1951.
Paris. Peace Conference, 1919.

Rules for entering the texts of official treaties are included in the section on Documents.

(b) International meetings (nongovernmental). (ALA, 132; p. 200-202) Meetings of conferences and congresses, international in character but private in membership, are entered preferably under the English name of the meeting if that form of the name has been used in the publications emanating from the meeting; otherwise the name in the prevailing language of the publications is used. The place or places and year of the meeting are included in the author heading of a conference that is held only once. If a session of a conference which meets several times is the corporate author for which entry is being made, the heading is extended to include the number, place, and year of the meeting.

International Conference on Adult Education, Helsingør, Denmark, 1949.
International Conference on Soil Science in the Mediterranean Region, Montpellier and Algiers, 1947.
International Conference of Wheat Experts. 2d (Preparatory) Rome, 1931.

(c) Institutes, conferences, and conventions (meetings). Publications issued by institutes, conferences, conventions, etc., are entered under the distinctive name given to the meeting itself, e.g., Southern Conference for Human Welfare; New England Newspapers Mechanical Conference.

If the meeting is associated with a particular place and date, these details are added to the author heading, e.g., Institute of State and Local Finance, Arlington, Va., 1950. Names of institutions at which meetings are held are also included in headings, e.g., Conference for Social Betterment, Blank College, Lynchburg, Va., 1950.

When no name can be found for the meeting, it is entered under the name of the place where the meeting was held, followed by a name "descriptive of the character of the meeting." (ALA, 135D; p. 203)

Syracuse, N.Y. Convention of Mechanics and Others, 1850.

(d) Committees and Commissions. (ALA, 139; p. 205-206) A committee or a commission, whether international, national, or local, if it is not under outside control, is entered under its own name as an autonomous corporate body. The name of the place in which its headquarters are located is added only when necessary for identification.

Committee on Public Administration Cases, Washington, D.C.
Commission on Hospital Care.
Citizens Committee for the Hoover Report.
Committee for Defense of Public Education, New York.
Commission on Financing Higher Education.

Names of committees and commissions appointed by a corporate body to perform designated functions are entered as a subhead under the name of the appointing authority.

American Council on Education. American Youth Commission.
Modern Language Association of America. Commission on Trends in Education.
Special Libraries Association. Committee on Microfilming and Documentation.

(e) Firms and corporations. (ALA, 144; p. 208-210) The entry for a firm or corporation is under its corporate name. The terms "incorporated" (inc.), "limited" (ltd.), and their foreign counterparts are added when such terms are part of the corporate name, e.g., McGraw-Hill Publishing Company, inc. These abbreviations are not italicized. When a firm name is identical with that of the personal name of the owner, the word "firm," is supplied in italics, following the inverted form of the name. The place name at the end of the firm name is omitted when the company has branches in several localities, e. g., Standard Oil Company. The word "Company" is not abbreviated in the corporate name of a firm.

> Wilson, H. W., firm. A proposed plan for printing Library of Congress cards in cumulative book form. [New York] 1946. 19 p. Z881.A1C35

B. Title as main entry. The heading under which a publication properly may be entered may be the title of the work. A guide to rules for title entries is provided in ALA, Index, p. 264.

The title is the logical choice for the main entry under circumstances such as those described below.

1. The author is unknown, as in an anonymous work for which the authorship has not been established.

2. A collection, made up of works by various authors, has a distinctive title useful for identification, and the editor plays an inconspicuous part in the creation of the collection.

3. The editorship of a continuing publication may change but the title remains the same and therefore provides the most reliable identification of the work.

4. A composite work has numerous contributors, no one of whom takes precedence as the final authority for the book, which therefore is best known by its title.

Types of material commonly entered under title include dictionaries, encyclopedias, almanacs, periodicals, newspapers, yearbooks, and directories. It is important to note, however, that the name of an individual editor or compiler takes precedence over the title as the main entry if the individual is sufficiently outstanding in connection with the publication to be considered responsible for it.

> The Editorial directory.
> Jahrbuch der Auktionspreise für Bücher und Autographen.
> The Philippine Islands; handbook of selected reference material.
> Who's who in our American government.
> The Harvard theological review.
> Bugle blast, an anthology from the services.
> Jack Aistroup and Reginald Moore, editors, 1943.
> The National encyclopedia. Editor in chief, Henry Suzzallo.

but
Cerf, Bennett A., and Henry C. Moriarty, eds. An anthology of famous British stories.

III. Body of the entry. (RDC, 3:2; p. 10) After the heading under which an item is to be entered has been established, the basic description of the work is supplied as the body of the entry.

Elements in description. (RDC, 3:5-14E; p. 12-26)

A. Title. The title is transcribed in the words of the title page.

1. Titles in more than one language. A title repeated in more than one language on the same title page is given in the first language used and also in English if that is the language of one of the succeeding titles, e.g., "Les Musées britanniques et la guerre. The museums of Britain and the war." A supplementary note names the different languages used if the text is repeated in the various languages, e.g., French, English, and German text.

2. Abridgment of the title is allowed in case of a long, discursive title except in the case of the descriptive bibliography which ordinarily indicates the physical properties of copies of rare books.

The opening word or words of the title are omitted in only two cases: (a) When the omission of the initial article makes possible the deletion of the author statement, e.g., "The works of John Adams," becomes "Adams, John. Works." (b) When the author's name in the possessive case repeats information supplied in the author heading, e.g., "John Adams' works" becomes "Adams, John. Works."

When abridgment occurs in the middle of the title it is indicated by the use of an ellipsis, but the omission of opening words of the title need not be shown by the three dots.

Any information eliminated by the abridgment of the title may be supplied in an annotation or note, if considered important.

Title page:

J. M. Nickell's botanical ready reference. Especially designed for druggists and physicians. Containing all of the botanical drugs known up to the present time, giving their medical properties, and all of their botanical, common, pharmacopoeal [!] and German common (in German) names. Comp. by J. M. Nickell. Chicago, Ill. [Printed by Ottaway and company] 1881.

Bibliographical entry:

Nickell, James M., comp. Botanical ready reference ... designed for druggists and physicians. Chicago [Printed by Ottaway] 1881. 268 p. RS164.N53

Gives medical properties and botanical, common, pharmacopoeial, and German common names of botanical drugs.

3. Additions. "Additions may be made to the title in the language of the title if it needs explanation and if brief statements to clarify it can be taken from the work itself." (RDC, 3:5C; p. 13)

Graham, Anthony W. Radio and television [since 1945] London, C. Cameron, 1952. 130 p.

If, however, an annotation is supplied, the additional information frequently may be incorporated in the annotation.

4. Supplied titles. If a title must be worded and supplied by the bibliographer, "the nature and scope of the contents of the work are described as briefly as intelligibility permits," e.g., Illinois, Governor. [Messages to the General Assembly]. (RDC, 3:5D; p. 13) Note the use of brackets to enclose such a title.

5. Alternative titles are retained because publications are best known by them in some instances, e.g., The land of forgotten people; or, Henry A. White's explorations in the valleys of the Amazon.

6. A subtitle which adds to the information contained in the title proper is included in the entry, e.g., Religions égyptiennes antiques; bibliographie analytique (1931-1943). Wordy and repetitious subtitles are dropped; the essential information that such subtitles may contain is provided in a supplementary note.

7. Translations of titles ordinarily are not provided if the original titles are given in one of the more familiar European languages, i.e., French, German, Italian, Spanish, etc. If, however, the translation of a title is supplied, it follows the original and is enclosed in brackets.

   The decision to provide or not to provide translations of titles throughout all or some of the entries for foreign titles in the same bibliography is determined by various considerations. These include the character of the compilation, the audience to which it is addressed, etc. An explanation of the policy adopted is therefore included with other explanatory statements in the preface, if necessary.

8. Transliteration of titles in non-Latin alphabets. Titles of books in Arabic, Bulgarian, Greek (modern), Hebrew, Russian, Serbian, Ukrainian, and Yiddish are transliterated by the use of tables in ALA, p. 243-249. Specifications for transliterating the Macedonian alphabet, the alphabets of the languages of Ceylon, India, Pakistan, and a transliteration table for Sanskrit using the Devanāgāri alphabet are found in CS, no. 31, Jan. 1954: 1-4. The system used for romanizing Chinese titles is known as the Wade-Giles method.[5] A "modified Hepburn" system is followed in the romanization of Japanese titles.[6] Korean titles are romanized according to the McCune-Reischauer plan.[7] If an English translation made from the original language is given after a transliterated title, it is enclosed in brackets.

B. Author statement. (RDC, 3:6; p. 14) Since the author statement following the title usually repeats information already available in the author heading, it is dropped when possible. However, it is included as a necessary part of the description under a variety of circumstances. These include: (1) grammatical correctness and clarity; (2) addition of names of important joint authors when these are represented by "and others" in the author heading; and (3) inclusion of a pseudonym or variant form of an author's name not used in the author heading.

Raymond, Charles B. Self-portrait, taken from the letters and journals of Charles B. Raymond.

Simmons, James S., and others. Global epidemiology, a geography of disease and sanitation, by James Stevens Simmons, Tom F. Whayne, Gaylord West Anderson, and Harold Maclachlan Horack.

---

[5] Giles, Herbert A. Chinese-English dictionary. 2d ed., rev. and enl. London, B. Quaritch, 1912. 1711, 84 p. PL1455. G62 1912a

[6] Kenkyusha's new Japanese-English dictionary. Takenobu Yoshitaro, general editor. American ed. Cambridge, Mass., Harvard University Press, 1942. p., [i]-iv. PL679. K4 1942

[7] McCune, George M., and E. O. Reischauer. The romanization of the Korean language based on its phonetic structure. In Royal Asiatic Society of Great Britain and Ireland. Korea Branch, Seoul. Transactions. v. 29; 1939. Seoul. p. 1-55. AS559. R7, v. 29

C. Edition. (RDC, 3:1A, p. 9; 3:7, p. 15; 3:10, p. 16) An edition has been defined as: "One of the successive forms in which a . . . text is issued either by the author or by a subsequent editor." (ALA, p. 231) "Different editions are most commonly distinguished by the difference in their imprints." (RDC, 3:10; p. 16) Variations between successive editions, the probable correction and enrichment of later editions, change of emphasis represented by deletions, and timeliness or the lack of it in an edition are matters which vitally affect the value of an item. For that reason the edition statement in a bibliographical reference is of prime importance to the user and therefore also to the compiler of a bibliography.

1. Edition statement. Statement of the edition follows the author statement, or in the absence of the latter, the title. No statement of "1st ed." is made unless the work is rare or significant because of special features. In a bibliography on a subject of current interest, the practice is to enter the latest published edition.

2. Form of statement. A numbered edition is described by the appropriate ordinal numeral followed by the suitable abbreviation of the vernacular word for "edition," e.g., 2d ed. (not 2nd ed.); 4th ed.; 3. Aufl; 4. éd., etc. Note that the numeral is followed only by a period and the abbreviated word for edition in entries for foreign works. If the edition is not numbered but is distinguished by descriptive words, these are used if possible in abbreviated form, in the edition statement, e.g., New ed., rev. and enl.; album ed. (See RDC, Appendix III, p. 121-124, Abbreviations.) When volumes that compose a set vary in edition from volume to volume, the editions and imprint dates are supplied in an informal note or as part of the contents note, whichever is simpler: e.g., Contents.--v. 1-2, Geography and biography. 2d ed. 1921.--v. 3-4, Science and literature. 3d ed. 1927.

Calot, Frantz, and Georges Thomas. Guide pratique de bibliographie. 2. éd., refondue avec le concours de Clément Duval. Paris, Delagrave, 1950. 278 p. (Bibliothèque des chercheurs et des curieux)
Z1035.C16 1950

Kohn, Pinchas J. Rabbinischer Humor aus alter und neuer Zeit, eine Sammlung von Anekdoten und "guten Wörtchen." 2., verm. Aufl. Frankfurt am Main, J. Kauffmann, 1930. 272 p. PN6231.H4K6 1930

Morison, Samuel E., and Henry S. Commager. The growth of the American republic. [4th ed., rev. and enl.] New York, Oxford University Press, 1950. 2 v. maps.
E178.M85 1950

Winchell, Constance M. Guide to reference books. 7th ed. Chicago, American Library Association, 1951. 645 p. Z1035.W79 1951
Based on the Guide to reference books, sixth edition, by Isadore Gilbert Mudge.

3. Successive editions. If successive editions of a work are cited in the same bibliography they are counted as separate items and are entered below the entry for the edition to which reference is first made. The order of entries for successive editions may be chronological by date from the earliest to the latest, or from the latest to the earliest, in reverse order. The choice of order depends upon the purpose of the bibliography, which determines the relative importance of indicating historical sequence or currency of revision of editions. The author heading and the title are not repeated before the edition statement of successive editions. Instead, two series of five hyphens each are used in substitution respectively for the author heading and the title. If the bibliography is printed, these two series of hyphens become two dashes (the first 2 ems, the second 3 ems in length) as on a printed catalog card where the same form is used to indicate supplements, etc. Other details of the bibliographical description are provided as usual.

Channing, Edward. A students' history of the United States. New ed. with additions. New York, Macmillan, 1898. 615 p. E178.1.C461

----- ----- 3d rev. ed. New York, Macmillan, 1913. 601 p. E178.1.C466

----- ----- 5th rev. ed. New York, Macmillan, 1924. 628 p. E178.1.C4672

The bibliographer, for reasons of clarity and economy of space, may prefer to incorporate the information concerning different editions of a publication in a statement to be included in the annotation, e.g., A third rev. ed. (1913, 601 p. E178.1.C466) and a fifth rev. ed. (1924, 628 p. E178.1.C4672) were also published by Macmillan.

D. Imprint. An imprint (place, publisher, and date) of a work cited in a bibliographical entry is significant for several reasons. It not only aids in completing a description of the item, but also gives the source from which copies may be secured if the work is still in print. The date of publication shows the timeliness of the work in relation to the subject of the bibliography.[8/] "The place of publication, particularly if it is not a large publishing center, may suggest a probable local viewpoint of the author. The publisher's name may also suggest a viewpoint or bias (especially when the publisher is a society or an institution) or may be an indication of the quality either of the subject matter or the physical make-up of the work." (RDC, 3:10; p. 16) When neither place of publication nor name of publisher is known, place of printing and name of printer may be used in the imprint if believed to be an aid of identification and location of the work.

1. Place. The place named in the imprint is that in which the publisher is located. Identification of the place is given by the name of the city alone, unless the name of a larger geographical unit is required for clarity or to distinguish between identical names, e.g., Washington, Pa. When publication takes place in a foreign location and also in the establishment of the same publisher in the United States, the names of both places are supplied only if the foreign location is named first in the publication, e.g., London, New York, Macmillan. But if the American place is named first in the publication, the foreign place name is omitted. If two or more places are given on the publication as the location of one publisher, only the first or the principal place is used in the imprint, unless a specific reason exists for naming other places.

2. Publisher. The name of the publishing agency is abbreviated as much as possible, while the demands of intelligibility are met, by the deletion of an initial article, words such as "and company," initials of first names of well-known publishers, and terms meaning "incorporated" or "limited," e.g., Fine Books Club; Scribner; Harper; Knopf; but Peter Smith; Oxford University Press; U.S. Govt. Print. Off. When a work is issued by several publishers in a country, only one name is given in the imprint. The one most significant in relation to the bibliography is chosen. When no distinction in importance is apparent, the first named publisher is chosen. In the case of two publishers, one American and one foreign, only the name of the publisher in the United States is given in the imprint, if that name appears first in the publication. Names of both publishers are given, however, if the foreign publisher is named first. When a work is published by one agency and distributed by another, the names of both are given, e.g., New York, American Literary Society; distributed by Columbia University Press, 1950.

[8/] Esdaile, Arundell J. K. A student's manual of bibliography. London, Allen & Unwin & The Library Association, 1931. (The Library Association series of library manuals, 1) p. 84-85. Z1001.E75

a. Omission of publisher's name. If the corporate author of a work is also its publisher, the author heading is considered sufficient and the name of the issuing agency is not repeated in the imprint.

> U.S. Treasury Dept. Library. National income and wealth in the U.S. and in many countries abroad; references. [Washington] 1950. 78 p. Z7164.W4U5 1950

However, if publication is by a subsidiary part of the same agency, or with the collaboration of others, the author heading no longer provides the complete information and the imprint statement repeats that name and includes also the additional names to complete the identification of the true publisher.

> U.S. Bureau of Medicine and Surgery. Manual of educational and vocational counseling for use in rehabilitation program of the Medical Department, U.S. Navy. Washington, Bureau of Medicine and Surgery and Bureau of Naval Personnel, Navy Dept. [1945?] 23 p. UB363.A5 1945a

If identical author and publisher are named in different languages, both forms are given in the entry.

> International Federation of University Women. Lexique international des termes universitaires. [Paris] Fédération internationale des femmes diplomées des universités, 1939. 755 p. LB2331.I6

b. Inclusion of publisher's address. Works published privately by a personal author, or by a publisher not widely known, may be difficult to secure without a more specific address than that afforded by the usual imprint. Under such circumstances the street address may be supplied after the name of the publisher, but the zone number is omitted to prevent possible confusion between numbers. The words, "The Author," are substituted for the author's name as publisher, in the imprint.

> Blank, Mary. Memories of fifty years. Washington, The Author (1201 20th St., N.W.) 1943.

> The Decachord; a magazine for students and lovers of poetry. v. 1+ 1924+ London, Philippa Hole (31 Brick St., Piccadilly)

3. Date.

a. Copyright date. Both the date on the title page and the copyright date are given in the imprint if they differ.

b. Inclusive dates. Within the same century, the century number is not repeated in inclusive dates of publication of a multiple volume work, e. g., 1937-42. However, if the several volumes of such a work have not appeared in the chronological order shown by the inclusive dates given in the imprint, an addition may be made to indicate the irregularity, e. g., 1921-30 [v. 1, 1930]; or the information may be given in an annotation.

E. Collation. A statement of the extent of a work in pages, leaves (text on one side of a sheet), or volumes, important illustrative material, and, if necessary, size, constitute the collation. In the following paragraphs the word "leaves" is to be substituted throughout if the work to be described has foliation rather than pagination.

1. Text complete in one volume. Ordinarily only the final pagination, omitting count of introductory pages bearing roman numerals, is used to indicate the extent of the text, e. g., 369 p., not 2 p. 1., iii-ix, 369 p. If the last page is not numbered, the appropriate number is supplied in brackets. When the importance of several sections of the text is indicated by their content or extent, sectional as well as final pagination is given, e. g., cxxxii, 850, 75 p.

2. Complicated pagination. Variously paged or unpaged works having less than 100 pages are described by recording in brackets a count of the total number of pages. Irregular pagination of longer works is indicated by giving the total pagination of the longer sections and adding in brackets the count of the total number of pages in the remaining sections, e. g., 151, 175, [35] p. Loose-leaf publications, if designed to receive additions, are always described as 1 v. (loose-leaf). Lengthy works with pagination too complicated to repay detailed description are designated as being in 1 v. (various pagings). In the last case a note may be added to explain the character of the variations.

3. Text in more than one volume.

a. The statement of the total number of volumes in a work published in more than one volume replaces the statement of pages in a one volume work, e. g., 10 v. Occasionally the character of the work, whether brief or encyclopedic, is significantly suggested by the number of pages in each volume. The pagination is then added to the statement of volumes, e. g., 2 v. (35, 28 p.); 2 v. (1015, 963 p.). If the work is paged continuously, the pagination is given in parentheses after the number of volumes, e.g., 2 v. (965 p.).

b. If a volume or a part of a work in multiple volumes is to be entered in a bibliography, one of the following methods may be used, depending upon the significance of the work to the particular bibliography.

(1) When one volume only is to be entered, the volume[9] number and the title of the individual volume, if any, precede the imprint. Pagination of the volume is shown in the collation statement.

> Edel, Leon J. Henry James. [v. 1] The untried years, 1843-1870. Philadelphia, Lippincott [1953] 350 p. PS2123.E33, v. 1

(2) If more than one volume, but less than the whole set, is to be described, the total number of volumes in the work is indicated in the collation statement, and attention is directed to the appropriate volumes in the note or annotation.

> Schneider, Georg. Die Schlüsselliteratur. Stuttgart, Hiersemann, 1951-53. 3 v. Z1026.S4
> See Bd. 1, Das literarische Gesamtbild, and Bd. 2, Entschlüsselung deutscher Romane and Dramen.

(3) When attention is directed to all volumes of a work that is in process of publication, an open entry may be preferable, giving volume number with a plus sign preceding the imprint, date of publication of first volume also with a plus sign, and no collation statement.

> Jefferson, Thomas, Pres. U.S. Papers. Julian P. Boyd, editor. v. 1+ Princeton, Princeton University Press, 1950+ E302.J463
> First 4 volumes cover 1760-1781. The extent of the work when completed is estimated at 50 volumes.

If information concerning the anticipated extent of a set in process of publication is easily available and appears significant, an annotation may be used to cover these data and possibly the

---

[9] Abbreviations are used for volume designations in this position, and they are given in the vernacular.

contents of the existing volumes or of any cited (see preceding) example).

4. Illustrative matter. Maps, portraits, tables, facsimiles, diagrams, etc., are mentioned in a statement of collation only when they are a feature of the work, or when they have special significance for the purpose of the bibliography. Under other circumstances illustrative material is described under the general term "illustrations," using the abbreviation "illus."

5. Size. Measurements of size are never supplied unless a work cannot be properly identified without them. In very rare cases when size must be added to the collation statement, the rules to be followed are those in RDC, 3:14D, p. 25-26.

6. Atlases, plans, etc., accompanying volumes of text. When such volumes and portfolios of plates belong to a set but are not numbered consecutively with other volumes in the set, that fact is recognized in the collation statement, e.g., 10 v. and atlas (50 plates). However, if the atlas has a special compiler or differs from the set in ways requiring further description, it is given a form of entry corresponding to that of a supplement. (See section on Supplements.)

7. Abbreviations. Terms used in the statement of collation, e.g., v., p., port., diagr., facsim., etc., are abbreviated in accordance with the list provided in RDC, Appendix III, p. 121-124.

IV. Series note.

A. Definitions.[10]

1. Series. "1. A number of separate works, usually related to one another in subject or otherwise, issued in succession, normally by the same publisher and in uniform style, with a collective title which generally appears at the head of the title page, on the half title, or on the cover..."

2. Series note. "In a catalog or a bibliography, a note stating the name of a series to which a book belongs. The series note ordinarily follows the collation."

---

[10] American Library Association. Editorial Committee. Subcommittee on Library Terminology. A. L. A. glossary of library terms, with a selection of terms in related fields; prepared by Elizabeth H. Thompson. Chicago, American Library Association, 1943. p. 124. Z1006.A5

B. Significance. A series note is significant as an aid in identifying and locating an item; for indicating its connection with other publications on the same subject, or related subjects, which the reader may wish to consult also; and as documentation for the authority and purpose of the work.

C. Elements. A series note may include as many of the following elements as are found in the series being described: (1) author; (2) title; (3) important editor; (4) number of item in a given series; (5) statement of the subseries to which the work also belongs; and (6) number of item in the subseries.

D. Form. Parentheses are used to enclose the series note, which follows the collation. Arabic numerals are substituted for roman numerals in stating the number of the item within its series, except when two numbers come together and are indistinguishable unless roman numbering is retained for one of them. The number of the item is given after the title of the series, either without punctuation or following a comma, in whichever way best expresses the numbering of the piece itself, e.g., (Collana legislativa e administrativa, 20); (U.S. Bureau of Labor Statistics. Bulletin no. 1063). Terms such as "Half-title," and "On cover," which are used to indicate the location of the series statement within the work itself, are not included in the note. Elements supplied by the bibliographer from a source other than the piece are enclosed in brackets.

E. Corporate body as author of the series not of the item. If the series has a corporate author that is not the author of the reference cited in the bibliography, the name of the corporate body is included in the series note under two circumstances: (1) the name of the author and the title are integrated in the series statement, e.g., (Publications de la Faculté des sciences économiques et sociales de l'Université de Genève, v. 11); and (2) the series cannot be properly identified without its author's name, e.g., ([Virginia] State Board of Education. Bulletin, v. 33, no. 9). The name of a corporate author, when present, is given in the form used in an author heading.

F. Author of series and of item identical. When the personal or corporate author or authors of the item and of the series to which it belongs are the same, the appropriate possessive pronoun is substituted for the author's name in the series note, e.g., (His Shadwell essays, v. 3); (Their International relations studies, no. 10); (Its Works in the humanities, 30).

G. Works in more than one series. (RDC, 3:16C; p. 33) When a work is issued in two series, one of which is a subseries of the other, both are included in the series note, the subseries in the second place.

> U.S. Dept. of State. Office of Public Affairs. The U.S. Foreign Service; a career for young Americans. Washington, Department of State, 1952. 22 p. (U.S. Dept. of State. Publication 4559. Department and Foreign Service series, 28)
> JX1705.A2884 1952

If the work is a part of more than one series issued by the same corporate body, and one series can be identified as more extensive than the other or others, the more extensive series is recorded without parentheses but with brackets, if necessary, as the first supplementary note. It is not added to the series note which follows the body of the entry.

Gt. Brit. Treaties, etc., 1936-1952 (George VI) Agreement between the Government of the United Kingdom of Great Britain and Northern Ireland and the Government of the Italian Republic for the prolongation of patents for inventions, London, 16th June, 1951. London, H. M. Stationery Off., 1951. 5 p. ([Gt. Brit. Foreign Office] Italy, 1951, no. 1) Law

[Gt. Brit. Parliament. Papers by command] cmd. 8305.

English and Italian text.

Brumm, John M. Health programs in collective bargaining. [A revision. Urbana, University of Illinois, 1951] 23 p. (Illinois. University. Institute of Labor and Industrial Relations. I. L. I. R. publications. Bulletin series, v. 3, no. 1)

University of Illinois bulletin, v. 49, no. 12.

H. Pamphlets published serially. Miscellaneous pamphlets issued serially, but monographic in the sense that individual issues are devoted to a single subject, at the discretion of the bibliographer may be entered under the body responsible for the serial, rather than under the author or the title of the pamphlet. The relationship of the individual item to the serial of which it is a part may then be indicated by a series note.

The American Forum of the Air. How can we combat corruption in government? Washington, Ransdell, 1952. [12] p. (Its Proceedings, v. 15, no. 31, Aug. 1952)

PN6072. A45, v. 15, no. 31

Participants: Oscar Chapman, Secretary of the Interior; U. S. Senator John Williams; and Frank Blair, general moderator.

Carnegie Endowment for International Peace. Issues before the sixth General Assembly. [Ann Winslow, editor] New York, 1951. 383-509 p. (International conciliation. Oct. 1951, no. 474) JX1907. A8, no. 474

Editorial Research Reports. Future of light metals, by Frank P. Huddle. Washington, 1946. 3-16 p. (Editorial research

Editorial Research Reports. (cont.) reports, Jan. 4, 1946, v. 1)[11/] H35.E35 1946, v. 1

National Education Association of the United States. Research Division. Schools and the 1950 census. Washington, 1951. 135-171 p. (Its Research bulletin, v. 29, Dec. 1951) L13.N477, v. 29

Newsweek Club and Education Bureaus. Security and freedom: the twofold challenge. New York, 1952. [21] p. (Platform, Apr. 1952) HS2501.P5, Apr. 1952

Public Affairs Committee. Blood's magic for all, by Alton L. Blakeslee. New York, 1948. 32 p. (Public affairs pamphlet no. 145) RM171.B58, no. 145

V. Call number and location symbol.

A. The Library of Congress call number assigned to a publication (or its location symbol) is placed at the right, at the end of the main block of the bibliographical entry. (See examples of entries at the end of Pamphlets Published Serially.) It is supplied as an aid to the identification of the work and as a means of securing access to it with minimum effort and likelihood of error. Not infrequently two copies of the same publication receive different call numbers, one copy perhaps being placed with the series to which it belongs, the other classified according to the immediate subject of which it treats. In such cases, both call numbers are recorded in the entry. Care must be taken to include all details of each call number, since certain preliminary and supplementary parts supply data essential to the location of the item, perhaps in a special collection, or as one part among many, e.g., Microfilm HD-19; QL461.I67 1948; Z673.I59, v. 10; and N400.M5 Suppl. 1939.

B. Location symbol. In the absence of a call number, or to provide a clue to the location of additional copies, a location symbol or symbols should be added in the following situations:

1. Location in the Library of Congress. For certain current documents, serials not yet completely cataloged, and special materials in the keeping of various divisions of the Library, no formal call numbers are available. The location of such items is indicated by inserting, in the

---

[11/] In this particular series note, the order of date and volume statements is reversed, because volumes are numbered 1 and 2 within each year, not in consecutive order throughout all years of publication.

position of the call number, a symbol designating their present location, e.g., Law (Law Library); GPRR (Government Publications Reading Room); SD (Serials Division); and Orientalia (Orientalia Division).

2. Location outside the Library of Congress. For works not in the collections of the Library of Congress, but attributed to other libraries by the National Union Catalog, the symbols used in that catalog constitute location symbols.[12] In the case of an important or scarce item, the symbols of several libraries may be given in the bibliographical citation. Attention is called particularly to the necessity of identifying location symbols in a preliminary section of the bibliography entitled "Key to Symbols."

VI. Supplementary notes are used in a bibliographical entry to supply data usually found within the work itself, but not susceptible to adequate description within the formal limits provided by the heading and the body of the entry. Such notes, if written to excess, tend to make an entry over-elaborate, thus detracting from its clarity. The bibliographer is therefore advised to evaluate them in relation to the effect they may have on the whole entry and to omit those that are not significant for the purpose of the bibliography. Supplementary notes are divided into two classes, known respectively as conventional notes and informal notes.

A. Conventional notes. (RDC, 3:15, p. 27-28; 3:16-24, p. 31-41) Notes that may be expressed in a prescribed formula are known as conventional notes. They provide significant information about the item in a variety of connections, as, for example: (1) the series of which the work is a part (see section on Series Note); (2) the names or other records found at the head of the title on the title page or on the cover, which may indicate, among other things, a sponsor of the publication whose relation to the work is not otherwise defined; (3) the identification of the work as an academic dissertation; (4) the statement of the "partial contents" or complete "contents" of the item, to extend its description, for a better understanding of its scope; and (5) the amplification of an author's name which has appeared in the heading of the entry in an abridged or changed form.

On cover: Headquarters Army Air Forces.

At head of title: Library of Congress, Union Catalog.

Inaug.-Diss.--Munich.

---

[12] U.S. Library of Congress. Union Catalog Division. Symbols used in the Union Catalog of the Library of Congress. [5th ed.] Washington, 1953. 65 p. Z881.A1U5 1953

Thesis (M. A.)--Georgetown University.

Contents. --La torre de los alucinados, por A. R. Valle. --Máscara del que duerme, por S. Salazar Bondy. --Agonía del amor, por D. Quiroz-Malca. --Los cantos elementales, por L. Nieto. --Marianita Coronel, por L. Valle Goycochea.

B. Informal notes. There is no set form to follow in the preparation of informal notes, which are phrased according to the bibliographer's best judgment. Since the information they contain varies item by item, it necessarily follows that a similar variation will prevail in the form used to convey such information. These notes are used chiefly for two purposes: (1) to contribute to the identification of the work; and (2) to describe or characterize the work and give its bibliographical history. Special features, such as bibliographies, translations, texts in different languages, and other editions, possibly under different titles, also may be indicated in notes. Titles of publications cited in supplementary notes and annotations are given in lower case except as rules for capitalization of titles require. (See Capitalization.) Quotation marks are used around titles of articles, chapters in books, etc. Titles of books and serials are italicized.

Microfilm copy made in 1949 by the Bibliothèque nationale. Negative.

Summary in English.

English and German text.

American ed. (New York) has title: Across to Norway.

Bibliographical references included in "Notes": p. [197]-222.

Translation of Quand j'étais montmartrois.

Bibliography: p. 290-320.

"The source of a quoted note is preceded by a dash, the source of a statement not quoted by 'Cf.' The source ... consists of the author's name, in direct form, and the title in sufficient fullness for identification without a key. Commonly used and easily recognizable words are abbreviated ... If page references are given, the source of the citation is specified by edition, or by place and date or publication." (RDC, 3:15A, p. 28)

C. Position of notes. The conventional series note is placed immediately after the collation, where it contributes helpfully to the identification of the piece.

If a note may be reduced to one word which therefore does not unduly extend the greatly condensed statements in the body of the entry, it may be placed after the collation or after the series note if there is one. Such notes include statement of frequency, e.g., "irregular," "quarterly," etc. Notes of frequency are not capitalized. The price of an item, if provided, is placed in the same position, e.g., "75 cents," as is the word "Typewritten," when that is appropriate. Ordinarily other notes are placed in planned order, beginning on the first line below the main part of the entry, with each note constituting a separate paragraph.

D. Order of notes. The order of notes is not mandatory, except that "at head of title," "bound with," and sequel notes are usually given first in order. A contents note, by reason of its length, fits best into the last position among the notes.

E. Notes in relation to annotations. A note, whether conventional or informal, is not to be confused with an annotation. The former is designed to amplify the formalized description given in the heading and the body of the entry. The latter has been defined as: "A descriptive extension of the title-page of a book in which the qualifications of the author, and the scope, purpose, and place of the book are indicated." To save space and achieve both conciseness and integration of information, supplementary notes may be coalesced with annotations at the discretion of the bibliographer. If this device is used, the result is an annotation, not a note. (See also Appendix C, Annotations.)

VII. Parts of books and other publications. The bibliographer frequently finds it necessary to cite part of a publication, although the remainder of the complete work may not be appropriate for inclusion. It becomes important, therefore, to devise a special form of entry, not only to identify the part itself, but also to provide bibliographical details that will establish the identity of the complete work, which must be known before the part can be located by the user. This form is known technically as an "analytic."

A. Form of entry. The part is entered first in the most conspicuous position, but the data provided consist only of the name of the author, if there is one, and the title of the selection. Next, a statement descriptive of the complete work is given following the word In: (a) author's name inverted, forename in full, followed by initials; (b) brief title; (c) edition, omitting editor's name unless particularly important in relation to the identity and authority of the publication; (d) imprint; (e) series note if any; (f) pages in which the part is found, omitting pagination or number of volumes of the complete work.

B. Typical usage.

1. Publications having various sections.

a. The work includes contributions by several writers and is paged continuously throughout.

Albright, William F. Some functions of organized minorities. In Conference on Science, Philosophy and Religion in Their Relation to the Democratic Way of Life. 5th, New York, 1944. Approaches to national unity; fifth symposium. New York, Distributed for the Conference by Harper, 1945. p. 260-275.

Handler, Joseph. Indo-China; eighty years of French rule. In American Academy of Political and Social Science, Philadelphia. Southeastern Asia and the Philippines. Philadelphia, 1943. (Its Annals, v. 226, March, 1943) p. 129-136.

Thorp, Willard L. Economic trends affecting credit. In Institute on Credit, Ohio State University. Proceedings. 1st; 1938. [Columbus] (Ohio State University publications. College of Commerce conference series, no. 4) p. 3-8.

b. The work of one author contains material on a variety of subjects, or on different aspects of one subject, so that a section, a chapter, one of a series of essays, a numbered part, certain consecutive pages, or other subdivision may be selected as the only citation in the complete work which is pertinent to the bibliography. If the part has no title, a brief descriptive title enclosed in brackets is supplied. The title of the complete work is preceded by In his, In her, In their, or In its (if the author of the complete work is a corporate body), as the case may require. If the entry includes a form subheading, such as U. S. Laws, statutes, etc., none of these forms is applicable; In is therefore followed by a repetition of the heading.

Jusserand, Jean J. A. A. The pardoners. In his English wayfaring life in the Middle Ages. 4th ed. London, Benn, 1950. p. 175-191.

Kent, Sherman. [A list of large, co-operative historical surveys] In his Writing history. New York, Crofts, 1941. p. 16n-17n.

Gt. Brit. Laws, statutes, etc. Compensation (defence) act, 1939. In Gt. Brit. Laws, statutes, etc. Requisitioned land and war works act, 1945, annotated and explained, by T. Mervyn Jones. London, Butterworth, 1945. p. 219-236.

If, however, the complete work merits inclusion, but a section is particularly significant, analytical treatment is not used. In such a case attention is called to the more important element in the book by means of a note, or as part of an annotation.

Hurt, Peyton. Bibliography and footnotes; a style manual for college and university students. Rev. and enl. by Mary L. Hurt Richmond. Berkeley, University of California Press, 1949. 167 p.
See particularly "Recommended form of reference to documents," p. 35-79, for a detailed treatment of documentary citations.

2. Articles in encyclopedias and other nonmonographic works in multiple volumes. An article in an encyclopedia, signed or initialed by the writer, is entered under his name. In the absence of a signature or identification of initials, entry is made under the title of the article. The following information concerning the complete work is supplied: (a) title of the encyclopedia; (b) edition statement;[13] (c) volume consulted; (d) place, publisher, and date of volume in question; and (e) reference to pages in which the article is found.

Burnett, Edmund C. Richard Henry Lee. In Dictionary of American biography. v. 11. New York, Scribner, 1933. p. 117-120.

Junta. In Diccionario enciclopédico Salvat. 2. ed. v. 8. Barcelona, Salvat, 1942. p. 383-385.

3. Serials that are parts of other serials. (See also section on Serials.) If analytical entry is desired for an important serial that is part of another serial, its description includes an author heading, if any, together with a brief title, followed by numbers of issues cited and dates covered. The description of the more inclusive serial which follows takes the place of collation, or imprint and collation, as in other analytical entries and includes the following details: (a) name of author if there is one; (b) brief title; (c) specific issues to which reference is made if numbered; (d) dates of issues cited; (e) imprint; and (f) a series note if necessary. When reference is made to a title in process of publication, statements of volumes and dates are left open, i.e., a plus mark is used without further

[13] If the edition applies only to the volume cited rather than to the whole work, the edition statement follows the volume number.

punctuation except second bracket, or final curve of parenthesis.

American Library Association. Handbook, [no. 5-44] 1907-47. In its Bulletin. v. 1-41; Jan. 1907-Dec. 1947. Chicago.

It is unnecessary to use an analytical form of entry if, as is frequently the case, an item may be described adequately by means of an informal note supplied in the entry of the larger work, or by a series note.

The Masterkey. v. 1+ May 1927+ Los Angeles, Calif., The Southwestern Museum. bimonthly.
Includes the museum's annual reports.

4. Articles in serials. Since general periodicals ordinarily may be identified through the use of widely available periodical indexes and union lists, it is considered unnecessary to give the bibliographical citation of an article published in such a periodical in analytical form following the word In. For such a citation, the author and title of the article are entered as in an entry for a book. The title of the periodical and other necessary details are supplied according to rules given in the section on Serials--Articles in Serials. If, however, the serial in which the article appears has a corporate author, or is issued in the form of proceedings, transactions, yearbooks, reports, and similar publications, an analytical type of entry is used (see Articles in Serials and Articles in Proceedings, Transactions, etc., in the section on Serials.)

VIII. Offprints, supplements, indexes, issues, etc. (RDC, 4:1-2, p. 43; 5:1-5:2, p. 45-46) In the course of compiling a bibliography it may be necessary to add to the entry prepared for a publication data concerning an offprint, supplement, etc. If such additions are relatively unimportant, they may be mentioned in an informal supplementary note, e.g., Statistical tables (10 p.) published as a supplement and inserted at the end. For more complete descriptions, the "dash" form is used below the completed entry for the item. In this form a series of five hyphens is substituted for the author's name. A similar series of hyphens is used if it is necessary also to represent the title. The description of the offprint, etc., follows the word offprint, reprint, or other appropriate term in sufficient detail for its identification. The call number is always included. These series of hyphens, employed in a processed bibliography with numerous items on a page, are substitutes respectively for the 2 em and the 3 em dashes used for a similar purpose on a printed catalog card.

A. Offprints (known also as reprints). If the original publication from which the offprint or reprint was made is available, the entry in the bibliography includes a reference to the larger work. Notes and an annotation, if required, follow the body of the entry. Then the "dash" form is used to introduce the offprint.

Evans, Luther H. The Library of Congress and its service to science and technology. College and research libraries, v. 8, July 1947: 315-321. Z671. C6, v. 8
----- ----- Reprint. [n.p., 1947] [315]-321 p.
E733. U6E826

Full imprint data for offprints and reprints is rarely available. No effort is made therefore to supply them. If neither place nor date of reprinting is known, "n.p." for "no place," and "n.d." for "no date" are used. The fact that no publisher is named is not indicated.

In the absence of the original larger publication, the reprint is entered in the bibliography as a separate monograph. A supplementary note is supplied to indicate its relation to the larger work.

Evans, Luther H. The Library of Congress and its service to science and technology. [n.p., 1947] [315]-321 p.
E733. U6E826
Reprinted from College and research libraries, v. 8, July 1947: 315-321. Z671. C6, v. 8

B. Supplements and indexes may be listed in either of the two ways described in the foregoing section A. If either supplement or index has a distinctive title, or a separate authority is responsible for it, that information is supplied, following the second series of five hyphens, otherwise the word "Supplement" or "Index" is sufficient. Statements of imprint, collation, and call number follow.

Wisconsin. Highway Commission. Report of the Madison traffic survey; a study conducted jointly by the State Highway Commission of Wisconsin and the city of Madison in Cooperation with the Bureau of Public Roads, U.S. Dept. of Commerce. [Madison] 1951. 2 v. illus., maps. HE372. M28 1951
----- ----- Traffic information supplement. [Madison] 1951. 1 v. (various pagings) illus., map.
HE372. M28 1951 Suppl.

When the supplement has an author and title different from that of the original work, and by its nature constitutes a separate monograph, it is entered as an additional item in a bibliography. An annotation may be used to explain its character as a supplement.

C. Issues. If variations between issues are so great that the publications cannot be considered exact copies but the title and the text of the works are the same, they are entered as different issues. Two series of hyphens are added followed by the phrase "Another issue" and the specification of bibliographical details which differentiate the issues.

D. References located in more than one source also may be indicated in the two ways described in A above. If an informal note is used to supplement the information in the original entry, it may read: Also published in Archives and libraries, v. 5, Sept. 1948. The "dash" form of entry, when adopted, is followed by statements of edition, imprint, and collation if reference is to a monograph. When a periodical reference is provided the title of the journal, volume, date, and pages are stated. Call numbers are also included in each case.

> Bush, Vannevar. As we may think. In his Endless horizons. Washington, Public Affairs Press, 1946. p. 16-38. Q171.B957
>
> Describes the possibility of a "memex," which will be "a device in which an individual stores all his books, records, and communications, and which is mechanized so that it may be consulted with exceeding speed and flexibility. It is an enlarged intimate supplement to his memory."
>
> ----- ----- Atlantic monthly, v. 176, July 1945: 101-108. AP2.A8, v. 176

E. Reviews and abstracts. References to reviews and abstracts of works cited in a bibliography may be profitably incorporated in annotations when these are supplied. Otherwise, they also are described in a subordinate position below the complete entry of the work to which they apply, but not in a form requiring dashes. Instead, the word Review or Abstract (italicized) is inserted, but not, as in the case of a note, indented in the form of a paragraph. The statements of author, title, source of publication, and call number in the Library of Congress follow.

> Schwegmann, George A., ed. Newspapers on microfilm, a union checklist. Philadelphia, Office of the Executive Secretary of the Association of Research Libraries, 1948. 176 p. Z6945.U52S33
>
> Reviewed by Preston W. Edsall of North Carolina State College in American archivist, v. 13, Jan. 1950: 72-74. CD3020.A45, v. 13

> Deutsche Gesellschaft für Dokumentation. Die Dokumentation und ihre Probleme. Leipzig, O. Harrassowitz, 1943. 205 p. Z1008.D485
> Review. Iben, Icko. Documentary reproduction in Germany. College and research libraries, v. 9, Apr. 1948: 180-183. Z671.C6, v. 9

F. Successive entries of different works by the same author (editor, compiler, or translator), personal or corporate, are ordinarily arranged in alphabetical sequence by title, but they may be arranged chronologically by date if that arrangement is better suited to the purpose of the bibliography. After the first entry the "dash" form of entry is substituted for the original author heading. If a new "dash" entry falls at the beginning of a second page, it is replaced by the full author heading, and the dashes are resumed for successive entries.

The indication of joint authorship is omitted from an author heading to be replaced by dashes. It is given instead only in the author statement in the body of the entry.

Corporate author headings, having identical subordinate parts, are nevertheless represented by five hyphens. If, however, the subordinate part changes, the whole corporate name is repeated. Names of joint corporate authors are represented in the author heading only by the first named corporate author.

It should be noted that these "dash" entries are not considered part of one entry but rather, as they are, independent references. When reference numbers are assigned, for purposes of identifying and indexing each citation, these successive entries are numbered separately.

<u>Reference No.</u> <u>Author</u> <u>Title</u>, etc.

101 Nevins, Allan. America, the story of a free people by Allan Nevins and Henry Steele Commager. Boston, Little, Brown, 1942. 507 p. illus.
E178.N44

102 -----, <u>ed</u>. The greater city: New York, 1898-1948, ed. by Allan Nevins and John A. Krout. New York, Columbia University Press, 1948. 260 p. illus.
F128.5.N4
Contents.--Foreword, by G. A. Whalen.--Past, present and future, by Allan Nevins.--Framing the Charter, by J. A. Krout.--From Van Wyck to O'Dwyer, by Carl Carmer.--The city's business, by T. C. Cochran.--The social and cultural scene, by Margaret Clapp.

103 ----- The New Deal and world affairs; a chronicle of international affairs, 1933-1945. New Haven, Yale University Press, 1950. 332 p. (The Chronicles of America series, v. 32) E173.C58, v. 32
"Bibliographical note": p. 315-321.

Reference No.	Author	Title, etc.
501	U. S. Library of Congress. European Affairs Division.	The European press today. Washington, 1949. 152 p. PN5110. U6 1949
502	-----	Freedom of information, a selective report on recent writing. Washington, 1949. 153 p. Z7164. L6U6
503	U. S. Library of Congress. Reference Dept.	Iran; a selected and annotated list, compiled by Hafez F. Farman. Washington, 1951. 100 p. Z3366. U53 At head of title: Library of Congress. General Reference and Bibliography Division.

II. DOCUMENTS

Outline

II. DOCUMENTS

The citation of a document contains the same elements that are essential to the description of books, pamphlets and other monographic publications. However, the complexities of documents, mainly because of their origin and form, result in complicated author headings and involved series notes. The intricacies of these and other details make it advisable to supply statements of the applications of the rules for entering books.

I. Corporate author.

A. Heading. Publications of countries, states, cities, etc., are entered under the name of the country, state, city, or other official unit which is responsible for them except when the entry is under a personal name, as noted below, and in cases explained in ALA in the section on "Government Publications." (ALA, 72-90; p. 126-148)

> United States. The mutual security program for fiscal year 1952; basic data supplied by the executive branch. Printed for the use of the House Committee on Foreign Affairs and the Senate Committee on Foreign Relations. Washington, U.S. Govt. Print. Off., 1951. 78 p. UA12.U52 1952
> At head of title: 82d Cong., 1st sess. Committee print.

B. Subheadings are italicized, and they are capitalized in compliance with the section on Capitalization.

1. Government agencies. Publications issued by executive departments, ministries, etc., are entered under the agencies as subheadings to the country, state, etc. (ALA, 72A, 75B; p. 126-127, 131)

   Canada. Dept. of Insurance.
   Gt. Brit. Ministry of Health.

2. Bureaus and offices within an executive department are entered as subheadings under the country, state, etc., not as subheadings to the department unless the name of the bureau or office is not distinctive. (ALA, 75A; p. 131)

   U.S. Bureau of Labor Statistics.
   not
   U.S. Dept. of Labor. Bureau of Labor Statistics.

3. Divisions and similar units which are subordinate to executive departments, ministries, bureaus, etc., are entered as subheadings to the departments, ministries, bureaus, etc. (ALA, 75B; p. 131)

   U. S. Library of Congress. General Reference and Bibliography Division.

4. Administrative or routine reports by an official of a government agency are entered under the agency, and the name of the author is given in an author statement. (ALA, 75C(1); p. 132)

5. Collection of reports. A collection or series of reports to a government agency, by different persons, is entered under the agency, and the names of the authors are given in the author statement. (ALA, 75E; p. 133)

6. Official commissions and committees are entered as subheadings under the jurisdiction or under the appointing department, legislative body, etc. (ALA, 81; p. 136-137)

   Kentucky. Legislative Research Commission.
   U. S. Bureau of Plant Industry. Committee on Southwestern Cotton Culture.

7. Laws, decrees, etc., are entered with the form subheading "Laws, statutes, etc." under the country, state, etc. (ALA, 84; p. 137-139) Only the first word of this subheading is capitalized.

   Oklahoma. Laws, statutes, etc. Compilation of narcotics laws, State of Oklahoma, prepared by Research Dept., State Legislative Council. Oklahoma City, 1951. 13 l. Law

   U. S. Laws, statutes, etc. Natural gas act. Washington, U. S. Govt. Print. Off., 1950. 48 p. Law
   At head of title: Federal Power Commission.

   ----- Title I, Public act no. 2, 73d Congress, and laws supplemental thereto, as amended, granting benefits to veterans and their dependents. Washington, U. S. Govt. Print. Off., 1950. 80 p. Law
   At head of title: 81st Cong., 2d sess. House committee print no. 302.

In this manual no effort is made to reproduce rules given in style manuals designed for use by specialists in legal bibliography. However, since it is occasionally necessary to include in a general bibliography references to specific laws published either as "slip laws" or in the United States

Statutes at Large, the information that such a citation should include is summarized as follows:

Heading. U. S. Laws, statutes, etc.

Title. Either the full form as printed, or a "short title" if one is designated in the law. It is desirable to supply the popular title in an annotation when it is known to the bibliographer.

Date. That of the approval of the law.

Series note. Details as follows: "Public law" or "Public no.," whichever form appears on the law, followed by the number of the law; United States Congress abbreviated to "Cong." preceded by the suitable ordinal numeral, without the number of the session since laws are numbered consecutively throughout the whole Congress; number of the volume of the Statutes followed by the abbreviation "Stat."; the page numbers, e.g., (Public law 75, 80th Cong., 61 Stat. 103-105).

It should be noted that currently these details are supplied on the "slip law" when it is originally published as well as in the Statutes.

U. S. Laws, statutes, etc. An act to authorize the printing and mailing of periodical publications of certain societies and institutions at places other than places fixed as the offices of publication. Approved Feb. 20, 1954. [Washington, U. S. Govt. Print. Off., 1954] [1] p. (Public law 298, 83d Cong., 68 Stat. 17) Law

----- Federal food, drug, and cosmetic act. Approved June 25, 1938. Washington, U. S. Govt. Print. Off., 1938. [20] p. (Public no. 717, 75th Cong., 52 Stat. 1040-1059) Law

8. Bills are entered under the country, state, etc., with the form subheading "Laws, statutes, etc. (Bills)." In order to distinguish the proposed legislation it is necessary to include either in the body of the entry or in the notes the number of the bill or resolution and the number and session of the Congress in which it was introduced. Numbers are written in figures, and the abbreviations "Cong." and "sess." are used. The bibliographer usually gives in a note the name of the person who introduced the bill or

resolution and the committee to which it was referred. Resolutions also may be cited in this way.

U. S. Laws, statutes, etc. (Bills) A bill to designate a building site for the National Conservatory of Music of America, and for other purposes. [Washington, Govt. Print. Off., 1927] 2 p. ML200. 5. N2 1927a
At head of title: 70th Cong., 1st sess. H. R. 7006.
Introduced by Mr. Hamilton Fish. Referred to the Committee on Public Buildings and Grounds.

Alternative: Bibliographers may prefer to enter bills and resolutions under the country, state, etc., and the legislative body with the name of the house in which it was introduced as subheading. The reason for this preference is that many bills never attain the dignity and status of law. Usually they are introduced by members or by a group of members without, in most instances, any responsibility for the authorship, and they are printed or made available by the House in which they are introduced.

U. S. Congress. House. A bill to designate a building site for the National Conservatory of Music of America, and for other purposes. H. R. 7006, 70th Cong., 1st sess. [Washington, Govt. Print. Off., 1927] 2 p. ML200. 5. N2 1927a
Introduced by Mr. Hamilton Fish. Referred to the Committee on Public Buildings and Grounds.

9. Treaties, except collections of treaties of several countries.

a. Single treaties are entered under the party given first on the title page with the form subheading "Treaties, etc." The subheading is followed by the inclusive dates of administration or reign and the name of the executive incumbent at the time of signing. (ALA, 88A; p. 140-141)

Gt. Brit. Treaties, etc., 1936-1952 (George VI) Trade agreement between the Government of the United Kingdom of Great Britain and Northern Ireland and the Norwegian Government, London, 15th December, 1950. Ratifications exchanged at Oslo on 31st August, 1951. London, H. M. Stationery Off., 1951. 7 p. ([Gt. Brit. Foreign Office] Treaty series, 1951, no. 83) JX636 1892 1951, no. 83
English and Norwegian.

U. S. Treaties, etc., 1933-1945 (Franklin D. Roosevelt) Civil affairs, administration and jurisdiction in

Netherlands territory liberated by an Allied Expeditionary Force. Agreement between the United States of America and the Netherlands, signed at London May 16, 1944, entered into force May 16, 1944. [Washington, U. S. Govt. Print. Off., 1951] 9 p. (U. S. Dept. of State. Publication 4168. Treaties and other international acts series 2212)
JX235. 9. A32, no. 2212
English and Dutch.

b. Collections of treaties of one country with other countries are also entered under the country which is concerned in all the treaties with the form subheading "Treaties, etc." (ALA, 88D; p. 142)

U. S. Treaties, etc. Treaties, conventions, international acts, protocols, and agreements between the United States of America and other powers. Washington, U. S. Govt. Print. Off., 1910-38. 4 v. JX236 1910

c. Multilateral treaties or conventions signed at international meetings are entered under the name of the conference. (ALA, 88B; p. 141)

[International Conference on European Inland Transport, London, 1944-45] European inland transport. Agreement between the United States of America and other powers, signed at London, May 8, 1945. Washington, U. S. Govt. Print. Off., 1945. 35 p. ([U. S. Dept. of State. Publication 2387] Executive agreement series 458)
JX236 1929, no. 458
HE11. I55 1945c
English and French.

10. Embassies, legations, etc. Publications issued by embassies, etc., are entered under the nation that is being represented, which is followed by the name of the representing body. The names of the countries where embassies and legations are assigned should be included in the heading, and for consulates, the names of the cities where they are located. (ALA, 78; p. 135)

U. S. Embassy. Gt. Brit. Disarmament of the German aircraft industry. Joint report of Economic Objective Unit, Economic Warfare Division of American Embassy and Research and Analysis Branch, Office of Strategic Services, London. [London] 1944. 22 l. (R & A no. 3066)
UB250. U33, no. 3066a

Gt. Brit. Legation. Switzerland. British press news and comment. Press series. Berne. semiweekly. D731.G773

Issued by the Press Dept., British Legation, Berne.

Latest in L.C.: Dec. 15, 1951.

France. Consulat. Santo Domingo. Correspondencia del cónsul de Francia en Santo Domingo. Ed. y notas de E. Rodríguez Demorizi. Ciudad Trujillo, Editora Montalve, 1944+ F1931.F7

11. Collections of messages to legislative bodies, executive orders, proclamations, and similar documents of presidents, governors, sovereigns, etc., which cover more than one administration are entered under the country, state, etc., with the name of the office as subheading. (ALA, 73A; p. 128)

Illinois. Governor. [Messages to the General Assembly] 1809+ Springfield. J87.I32

U.S. President. Proclamations and orders relating to the National Park Service up to January 1, 1945. Compiled by Thomas A. Sullivan. Washington, U.S. Govt. Print. Off., 1947. 331 p. SB482.A3 1947

At head of title: United States Dept. of the Interior. National Park Service.

12. Single messages to legislative bodies, executive orders, proclamations, etc., of presidents, governors, sovereigns, etc., are entered under the country, state, etc., with the name of the office as subheading and with the name of the incumbent in parentheses. (ALA, 73B; p. 128-129)

Gt. Brit. Sovereigns, etc. (George VI) Order by His Majesty to amend the Order of the 27th September, 1949, concerning retired pay, pensions and other grants for members of the Air Forces and of the nursing and auxiliary services thereof disabled, and for the widows, children, parents and other dependants of such members deceased, in consequence of service after the 2nd September, 1939. London, H. M. Stationery Off. [1951] 5 p. ([Gt. Brit. Parliament] 1951. House of Commons. [Reports and papers] 196)

13. Legislative bodies. Reports, proceedings, etc., of legislative bodies are entered under the country, state, etc., with the name of the body as subheading. (ALA, 74; p. 130-131)

Gt. Brit. Parliament. House of Commons. Reports from committees. v. 2; 1824. Artizans and machinery: six reports of minutes of evidence. [London] 624 p. (Its Sessional papers, 1824, v. 5) J301. K6 1824, v. 5

Michigan. Legislature. Joint Committee to Study Foster Care. Foster care of children in Michigan; report. Seven studies concerning foster care of children. [Lansing] 1951. 256 p. HV742. M5A54 1951

14. Constitutions are entered under the country or state with the form subheading "Constitution." (ALA, 85; p. 140)

Oregon. Constitution. Constitution of Oregon. Salem, E. T. Newbry, Secretary of State [1951?] 24 p.

II. Personal author. In the following instances documents are entered under the name of the author, compiler, editor, etc.

A. Nonadministrative publications. Scientific papers, addresses, and other publications not administrative or routine but issued by the agency of which the author, compiler, editor, etc., is an official.

MacLeish, Archibald. Deposit of the Magna Carta in the Library of Congress on November 28, 1939; remarks of Archibald MacLeish, the Librarian of Congress. [Washington, Library of Congress, 1939] 4 p. Z733. U57Z 1939c

B. Reports not by an official. Reports made to a government agency by a person who is not an official. (ALA, 75D; p. 132-133)

C. Parts of a series which have been entered under an official heading. (ALA, 75C(2) note; p. 132)

Solberg, Erling D. Rural zoning in the United States. Washington [U.S. Govt. Print. Off.] 1952. 85 p. (U.S. Dept. of Agriculture. Agriculture information bulletin, no. 59) S21. A74, no. 59

D. Single addresses and collected editions of papers of a president, governor, etc., (ALA, 73C; p. 129-130) with the exception of messages to legislative bodies, executive orders, etc., for which see Collections of Messages and Single Messages.

E. Collections of treaties of several countries. (ALA, 88C; p. 141)

Elliot, Jonathan, comp. The American diplomatic code embracing a collection of treaties and conventions between the United States and foreign powers: 1778 to 1834. Washington, Printed by J. Elliot, Jr., 1834. 2 v. JX231.E6

III. Joint authors. If more than one agency is responsible for a publication, it is entered under the agency named first in the work. As the names of the other agencies concerned often are indicative of the nature of the study or furnish some pertinent information, the bibliographer may wish to include those names either in the author statement or in a note or annotation. In this way it will be possible to index the item under all of the corporate authors and provide an additional key to the publication.

IV. The body of the entry. The description of a document in the body of the entry follows the same general principles as that for books. However, attention is directed to the following elements.

A. Author statement. When the name of the personal author, editor, or compiler is included in a publication which is entered under a government agency, the name of the author, editor, or compiler is given in the author statement. It may be necessary also to designate in the author statement or in a note or annotation the branch, section, or unit that prepared the publication; to show that another organization cooperated; and other important information.

China. Ministry of Information. China handbook, 1937-1945; a comprehensive survey of major developments in China in eight years of war. [Editor-in-chief: Hollington K. Tong] Rev. and enl., with 1946 suppl. New York, Macmillan, 1947. 862 p. DS777.53.A52 1947

U.S. Bureau of Foreign and Domestic Commerce. Office of Industry and Commerce. A source of new product possibilities for manufacturers; a partial listing of patents available for food machinery, equipment, devices, products and processes. Prepared by the Marketing Division in cooperation with the U.S. Patent Office. Washington, U.S. Dept. of Commerce, Office of Domestic Commerce, 1948. 60 p. TP373.U5 1948c

B. Imprint. If the name of the government agency in the author heading of an entry is exactly the same as that of the publisher, the issuing agency is omitted from the imprint since it would be understood. However, if a word in either name differs or if a subordinate part is included in one and not in the other, the publisher is given.

"U. S. Govt. Print. Off." is the abbreviation used in the imprint if the United States Government Printing Office is the publisher of an item issued since February 1927, but "Govt. Print. Off.," without "U. S.," for a publication prior to February 1927.

C. Series notes. When a document is a part of more than one series, each series is noted. A series subordinate to another is given in the second position. (RDC, 3, p. 33; see also section on Series Note in Books, Pamphlets, and Other Monographic Publications.)

V. Filing arrangement. When more than one item begins with the same word, which is the name of a place, the official publications entered under the place follow a name of a person and precede a title. (U. S. Library of Congress. Processing Dept. Filing manual. Washington, 1945. Order of Entries, Ord 1-6. Z696. U57)

France, Anatole.
France. Ministère des affaires étrangères.
France illustration.

VI. United States Congressional publications.

A. Heading. Publications for which the Congress of the United States is responsible are entered under "U. S." with the subheading "Congress."

U. S. Congress. Biographical directory of the American Congress, 1774-1949, the Continental Congress, September 5, 1774, to October 21, 1788, and the Congress of the United States from the 1st to the 80th Cong., March 4, 1789, to January 3, 1949, inclusive. [James L. Harrison, compiler] Washington, U. S. Govt. Print. Off., 1950. 2057 p. illus. (81st Cong., 2d sess. House. Document no. 607) JK1010. A54

B. Subheadings. The hearings, reports, documents, committee prints, etc., of a Congressional committee are entered under U. S. Congress with the appropriate subheading of House, Senate, Conference Committee, Joint Committee, etc. If a committee of the House or Senate is responsible for the publication, the committee is entered as a subheading under the House or Senate.

U. S. Congress. Joint Committee on the Economic Report. Increasing domestic wool production; wool consumption and production in the United States and programs needed to assure high level wool and sheep production. Washington, U. S. Govt. Print. Off., 1952. 12 p. (82d Cong., 2d sess. Senate. Document no. 100) HD9895. A54 1952b

U. S. Congress. House. Committee on Appropriations. State, Justice, Commerce and the Judiciary appropriation bill, fiscal year 1953; report to accompany H. R. 7289. [Washington, U. S. Govt. Print. Off., 1952] 38 p. (82d Cong., 2d sess. House. Report no. 1665)
HJ10. B3 1952

C. Hearings. An entry for hearings should include (1) the title of the hearings, (2) the number of the bill or bills (or resolutions) under consideration whenever mentioned, (3) the word "Hearing" or "Hearings," and (4) the number of the Congress and session. If the hearings were held "before a subcommittee" this statement follows the word "Hearings." It is unnecessary to repeat the name of the committee in the body of the entry unless there is a reason. The name of the chairman of the committee is included in the notes.

U. S. Congress. House. Committee on Interior and Insular Affairs. To revise the Organic act of the Virgin Islands. Hearings before the Subcommittee on Territories and Insular Possessions, 82d Cong., 2d sess., on H. R. 2644. Washington, U. S. Govt. Print. Off., 1952. 175 p.
HD171. A18A32
Monroe M. Redden, chairman of subcommittee.

D. Reports. Entries for reports include (1) the title of the report; (2) the bill number; (3) a series note containing the number and session of Congress, House or Senate, and publication number; and (4) a serial number whenever known.

U. S. Congress. House. Committee on the Judiciary. Providing for the appointment of additional circuit and district judges, and for other purposes; report to accompany S. 1203. [Washington, U. S. Govt. Print. Off., 1952] 98 p. (82d Cong., 2d sess. House. Report no. 1664)
JK1587. A52 1952
Serial no. 11576

U. S. Congress. Senate. Committee on Armed Services. National Security Training Corps act; report to accompany S. 2441. [Washington, U. S. Govt. Print. Off., 1952] 44 p. (82d Cong., 2d sess. Senate. Report no. 1205)
UB353. A543 1952
Serial no. 11566

E. Congressional Record. Since the Congressional Record is a serial publication, entries for it follow the general principles for entering serials with the following exceptions:

1. Heading. Entry is made under author whenever possible. In the case when a Senator or a Member includes, as an extension of his remarks, an article by another person, the item is entered under the name of the author of the article. The name of the Member or Senator is given in a statement following the title and source of the article.

   Sullivan, Mark. Root cause of labor troubles seen revealed by wire strike. An article from the New York herald tribune of Wednesday, Jan. 16, 1946. Extension of remarks of the Hon. Robert F. Rich, of Pennsylvania, in the House of Representatives, Jan. 16, 1946. Congressional record, 79th Cong., 2d sess., v. 92: A72.
   J11.R5, v. 92

2. Congressional remarks. The House of Congress in which the remarks were made and the date of their expression follow the title of the statement.

   Murray, James E. United Nations Educational, Scientific and Cultural Organization. Remarks in the Senate of the United States, Jan. 28, 1946. Congressional record, 79th Cong., 2d sess., v. 92: 439-443.
   J11.R5, v. 92

3. Congress and session must be included. In an entry for an article the date of the issue may be omitted if it appears elsewhere in the body of the entry, e.g., Statement in the Senate of the United States, May 24, 1945.

4. Issues. The Congressional Record is published in a daily issue, a semi-monthly issue, and a permanent, bound edition. The daily and the semi-monthly issues have the same paging but the bound edition has different paging. For this reason it is necessary to use terms that distinguish the unbound issues. Reference to articles in the bound volume is preferred but if there is need to cite current, unbound numbers, the words "daily ed." or "semi-monthly ed." are inserted in brackets following the title of the serial, e.g., Congressional record [daily ed.].

VII. League of Nations, United Nations, etc. Publications of the League of Nations, the United Nations, and other international groups are entered according to the general rules for describing documents. However, some basic adaptations are noted below:

A. Heading. Publications of these international bodies are entered under their respective names, e.g., League of Nations; United Nations Educational, Scientific and Cultural Organization; etc.

B. Subheadings. Assemblies, secretariats, councils, etc., are entered as subheadings under the organization.

C. Notes.

1. Series. If a United Nations publication is in a subseries and also in the United Nations Document series, the subseries is given in the series note, and the United Nations Document number, in a note. Document numbers assigned to a publication by another organization are also added to the notes.

2. Sales numbers are included in the notes when available.

3. Languages. If it is apparent that a publication is issued in other languages than the language of the issue cited, this fact is mentioned in the notes.

D. Illustrations of the important points noted above:

League of Nations. Assembly. First Committee. Proposed amendments to the rules of procedure of the Assembly; report. Rapporteur: M. Lange (Norway) [Geneva] 1935. 2 p. (A. 69. 1935. v) JX1975. A49 1935h
At head of title: Geneva, September 26th, 1935. League of Nations.

United Nations. Economic and Social Council. Economic Commission for Europe. Directory of building research and development organizations in Europe; prepared by the Secretariat of the UN Economic Commission for Europe and published jointly with the Housing and Town and Country Planning Section of the Dept. of Social Affairs. Geneva, 1951. 116 p. (UN series: Organizations concerned with building, housing and town and country planning) JX1977. A2 ST/SOA/Ser. H/4
United Nations [Document] ST/SOA/Ser. H/4. Sept. 1951.
"United Nations publications. Sales no.: 1951, IV. 5."

United Nations. Library. United Nations documents index. v. 1- Jan. 1950- [New York] monthly. (United Nations. Document)
Z6482. U45
JX1977. A2

United Nations Educational, Scientific and Cultural Organization. Dept. of Mass Communications. Division of Free Flow of Information. World communications, press, radio, film; report. [Paris, 1950] 220 p. (United Nations Educational, Scientific and Cultural Organization. Publication no. 700)
P90. U5

III. SERIALS

Outline

III. SERIALS

Serials are publications issued in successive parts, usually at regular intervals, and, as a rule, intended to be continued indefinitely. Because of the special characteristics of these publications, it is necessary to explain the adaptation of the general principles that govern entries for monographs to the description of serials.

I. Serials as a whole.

A. Heading. (ALA, 50; p. 10-14) Periodicals and newspapers are entered under the latest title. Ordinarily this also applies to a periodical issued by a society, institution, or government agency. However, if the title of a serial publication issued by a corporate body begins with a word that is not distinctive, such as "Journal" and "Bulletin," entry is made under the corporate author. In this case if the title contains the name of the author, the name is omitted from the title, e.g., "Royal Central Asian Society, London. Journal." A short title is generally used, and subtitles are omitted unless necessary for identification or for clarification of the scope of the publication (see RDC, 7:4; p. 52-53).

B. Body of entry.

1. Volume number and date follow the title or subtitle. The number of the part is omitted unless it is necessary for identification. On a Library of Congress catalog card the volumes and dates following the title indicate the holdings of the Library, and if the Library does not have the first issue no record is made in this position. (RDC, 7:5; p. 53-54) However, the bibliographer finds it more important to give the volume and date of the earliest issue in place of the statement of holdings following the title. If it is necessary to indicate Library of Congress holdings also, this information may be supplied in a note stating "L. C. has ," "L. C. lacks ," or "L. C. set incomplete."

a. Abbreviations and numerals. To achieve economy in editing printed catalog cards bibliographers in the Library of Congress follow the general rule that "abbreviations for terms used in volume designations and for months are given in the vernacular. Arabic numerals are used." (RDC, 7:5B, p. 53; p. 126-127) However, when English abbreviations seem more convenient, economical, consistent, or suitable, they may be used.

b. Punctuation. The volume number and date are separated by a semicolon unless there are two or more series of volume numbers; in this case, commas are used to separate volumes and dates, and semicolons are used between series. (RDC, 7:5C; p. 53-54) A plus sign is used after both volume and date to indicate that the serial is being published currently. If the date includes the name of the month, no punctuation is used immediately after the name unless it is abbreviated, e. g., May 1953; Aug. 1953.

> Amerasia. v. 1-11; Mar. 1937-July 1947. [New York] 11 v. in 15. DS501. A55
> Frequency varies.

> The Asiatic review. v. 1-10, Jan. 1886-Oct. 1890; 2d ser., v. 1-10, Jan. 1891-Oct. 1895; 3d ser., v. 1-34, Jan. 1896-Oct. 1912; new ser., v. 1+ Jan. 1913+ London, T. F. Unwin. quarterly. DS1. A7

> Europa. anno 1+ 30 apr. 1945+ Roma, Edizioni del lavoro. monthly. D1050. E87

2. Imprint of a serial consists of place of publication and publisher; in other words, the date is omitted if it is included in the statement following the title. The latest place of publication and the latest publisher are given. In the case of serials in foreign languages the place of publication is given in the vernacular. If the publisher is the same as the name in the title, it is not repeated in the imprint.

3. Collation. In case a serial is no longer publisher or if only certain volumes are cited, the total number of volumes is given after the imprint. If a serial is complete in one volume, the pagination is given. Occasionally it is desirable to show the average length of the volumes, and this may be indicated in a note by citing one volume, preferably the latest, with its pagination. Illustrative material is described for the whole set in the collation but features of certain volumes may be brought out in the notes or annotations.

C. Notes describing serial publications may be informal or they may be embodied in annotations. However, they are usually presented in a conventional style like those on the catalog cards. The following order is suggested. (RDC, 7:8; p. 55-61)

1. Frequency follows the collation if described in one word, e. g., quarterly; if a longer statement is necessary it is given in a note. (See entry for Amerasia under Punctuation.) When the title contains the frequency, repetition is not necessary, e. g., Monthly checklist of state publications.

2. Duration and suspension are stated in a note if not shown in the statement of holdings. When the authenticity of the data is questioned or

when the details concerning the volumes and dates are not available, the note position is preferred.

> al-Andalus. v. 1+ 1933+ Madrid-Granada. semi-annual. DP102. A6
> Publication suspended 1937?-39.

> The Uganda journal. London, Oxford University Press. semiannual. DT434. U2U3
> Began publication in Jan. 1934.
> Journal of the Uganda Society.

"No more published?" is noted when there is doubt as to whether the serial has ceased publication.

3. Connection with preceding publications. Usually the bibliographer feels that it is helpful to show in a note the continuity between a serial and its predecessor.

> Pan-Pacific. v. 1+ Jan. /Mar. 1937+ New York. quarterly. DU1. P18
> Supersedes the Mid-Pacific magazine.

Titles absorbed are indicated when they are significantly different and important.

> Extrême-Asie, revue indochinoise; revue mensuelle illustrée, organe du Bureau officiel du tourisme en Cochinchine. 1926+ Saigon (Indochina) Société "Extrême Asie." DS521. E8
> Absorbed Revue indochinoise and Revue du tourisme in July 1926.

Mergers of serials. In a bibliography it is seldom necessary to enter a serial that has been merged into another publication, for it is preferable to enter the latest title with a note stating that it absorbed the earlier serial.

4. Organ. If a serial is an organ of a society or organization it is important to note the fact.

> Industriários. no. 1+ fev. 1948+ [Rio de Janeiro] bimonthly. HD7106. B8I5
> Official organ of the Instituto de Aposentadoria e Pensões dos Industriarios.

5. Variations in title. The statement "title varies" or "subtitle varies" is generally used to avoid giving unnecessarily long bibliographical descriptions of changes of title. When the variations in title are important to the bibliography they are noted with the volumes or dates, if readily accessible.

> The China monthly review. v. 1/ June 9, 1917/
> Shanghai, China, Millard Pub. Co.
> DS501.C5
> Title varies: June 23, 1923-Aug. 5, 1950, The China weekly review.

6. Variations in corporate author are also indicated if considered valuable to the identification of the work or significant in relation to the subject of the bibliography. When available, dates and volumes of the period of variation are included.

7. Editors or persons connected in some way with the serial are named only if they are important to the identification of the publication or well known in the subject field covered by the bibliography.

> Population index. v. 1/ Jan. 20, 1935/ Princeton, N. J., Office of Population Research, Princeton University, and Population Association of America. quarterly. Z7164.D3P83
> Editors: July 1945/ F. W. Notestein, I. B. Taeuber, L. K. Kiser.

8. Variations in imprint are usually not recorded in a bibliography unless there is an important change in the name of the publisher.

> Handbook of Latin American studies. no. [1]/ 1935/ Gainesville, University of Florida Press, 1936/ annual. Z1605.H23
> Published in Cambridge, Mass., by Harvard University Press, 1936-47.

9. Contents notes generally bring out features common to all of the issues.

II. Special numbers are treated like monographs with the relationship to the regular numbers shown in the notes. (RDC, 7:10; p. 62) They are entered under the title of the serial unless an author can be determined. (ALA, 5C(3); p. 12)

III. Articles in serials. Entries for articles in serials differ from those for books and serials as a whole in that the title of the serial and information pertinent to it take the place of the imprint and collation.

A. Elements are arranged in the following sequence:

1. Author and title of the article are entered according to the same principles as those for books.

2. Title of serial is given as explained with reference to the heading for serials as a whole, except that if the title has changed, the one used at the time the article appeared is cited. The initial article "the" is omitted unless it is an integral part of the title. Words in the title are not abbreviated.

3. Place of publication is supplied if it is necessary as a means of identification. However, location is usually omitted if it can be easily found through use of standard reference sources. Some instances in which the place name is unnecessary are: (a) the periodical is well-known, (b) the information may be confusing rather than helpful to the user in cases of changed locations, and (c) the place is apparent from the author or title. If the place is given in the entry it is enclosed in parentheses following the title, and it is the city in which the serial was published at the date of the article.

4. Volume and date. The volume, designated by its abbreviation, and number are followed by the date of the issue, consisting of month (using abbreviated forms listed in RDC, p. 126), day, and year, e. g., Library journal, v. 79, Jan. 15, 1954: 107-115. When a new unnumbered series is referred to, the letters "n. s." precede the volume, e. g., Fortnightly, n. s., v. 150, June 1952: 16-50. If the number of the issue is also needed for identification, it is added after or in place of the volume number.

   Abbreviations of terms used for volumes and months in entries for articles in serials are similar to those in entries for serials as a whole in that they are given in the vernacular unless it is more convenient, economical, consistent, or suitable to use English. Numbers are given in arabic figures.

5. Pages are given in arabic figures following a colon, without the letter "p." If an article covers more than one page, the inclusive pagination is given without omission in the second number, e. g., 502-562. Full pagination is preferred rather than the plus sign or similar designation, e. g., 61-63, 70-72, 90.

6. Call numbers include the volume numbers and any details that may be necessary such as identification of the series, date of the serial if volumes are not numbered, and indication of a supplement, e. g., AS492. S3, 3d ser., v. 16; AP50. R3, n. s., v. 50; AP2. H4, July 1950; Z695. U4735 1949 Suppl.

B. When the word "In" is used. Entries for articles in serials include the word "In" only when reference is made to an article in a serial that is entered under author or is in proceedings, transactions, etc. (See Articles in Proceedings, Transactions, etc.) "In" is written in italics preceding the author of the serial. This use of "in" provides clear demarcation between the article and the author of the serial from which it is taken, thus eliminating confusion as to where one ends and the other begins.

Newspaper microfilming in the United Kingdom. Microfilm clearing house bulletin, no. 23. *In* U.S. *Library of Congress*. Information bulletin, v. 11, Sept. 15, 1952: appendix, 1-3. Z733.U57I6, v. 11

C. Punctuation of the elements that follow the heading and title of the article: The corporate author heading is followed by a period; title, by a comma, or by place, if given, within parentheses; volume number, by a comma; day, by a comma; year, by a colon; page numbers, by a period; a comma separates the call number proper from the volume number which is added to the call number. No punctuation is used immediately after the month unless the name is abbreviated, e.g., June 1950; Jan. 1951.

Complete books now published in microprint on index cards. Publishers' weekly, v. 154, July 24, 1948: 305-306.
Z1219.P98, v. 154

Huppert, Harry G. Korean occupational problems. *In* U.S. *Command and General Staff School, Fort Leavenworth.* Military review, v. 29, Dec. 1949: 9-16.
Z6723.U35, v. 29

[Indochina] France illustration, v. 5, June 4, 1949: 557-611.
AP20.F695, v. 5
Entire issue is devoted to Indochina.

Kang, Younghill. How it feels to be a Korean in Korea. United Nations world, v. 2, May 1948: 18-21.
JX1901.U54, v. 2

MacLeish, Archibald. UNESCO's task. *In* American Association of University Professors. Bulletin, v. 32, winter 1946: 605-609. LB2301.A3, v. 32

Thomas, Lewis V. Turkey: partner of the west. Foreign policy bulletin, v. 31, Aug. 1, 1952: 5-7.
E183.7.F72, v. 31

D. Continuations of a reference in several issues of the same serial may be combined but they should retain clarity. The following forms are suggested.

1. Continuous pagination with items in successive issues:

Smith, Isabel W. Chosen. National geographic magazine, v. 150, Apr.-June 1946: 560-590, 708-732, 859-899; v. 151, Jan.-Feb. 1947: 20-40, 90-120.
GN1.N27, v. 150, 151

2. Continuous pagination of issues with items in scattered issues:

New techniques. Library journal, v. 77, May 1, June 15-July 1952: 780-782, 1066, 1068, 1178, 1180-1181; v. 79, Jan. 15, 1954: 133-134.
Z671.L7, v. 77, 79

3. Separate pagination with items in successive issues:

Visiting our troops. Travel, v. 100, Apr. 1947: 18-22; May: 15-16; v. 101, Jan. 1948: 20-22; Feb.: 30-31.
G149.T73, v. 100, 101

4. Separate pagination with items in scattered issues:

The Librarian's conference. In U.S. Library of Congress. Information bulletin, v. 10, July 2, 1951: 5; July 23: 8; Aug. 20: 8; v. 12, Jan. 5, 1953: 4.
Z733.U57I6, v. 10, 12

IV. Articles in proceedings, transactions, yearbooks, reports, and similar publications issued serially are entered according to the general principles for analytical entries for books. However, the adaptations for entering serials as a whole are also taken into consideration, i.e., volume number and date follow the title; date is omitted from the imprint unless it differs from the date which follows the title.

Garnett, Maxwell. UNESCO. In The Year book of world affairs. v. 1; 1947. Edited by G. W. Keeton and Georg Schwarzenberger. London, Stevens, p. 202-223. JX21.Y4, v. 1

Stevens, S. K. State and local history in relation to national and international affairs. In Middle States Council for the Social Studies. Proceedings. v. 44, pt. 2; 1946-47. Philadelphia, 1948. p. 11-15. D16.3.A23, v. 44, pt. 2

APPENDIX A

ABBREVIATIONS, ALPHABETIZING, AND NUMERALS

ABBREVIATIONS.

I. Bibliographical entries.

A. Headings. Abbreviations are used in headings in accordance with a list found in ALA, p. 236-237.

B. Other elements of entries, notes, contents, etc. The list of abbreviations used in a bibliographical description, other than the heading, is found in RDC, Appendix III, p. 121-127. An accompanying statement of policy reads: "Abbreviations are used except in the recording of titles (including alternative and subtitles), whether these are in the body of the entry, the series note, list of contents, or cited elsewhere in the entry, and except in quoted notes. They need not be used if the brevity of the statement, or any other consideration, makes abbreviation in poor taste or if the resulting statement may not be clear. Single letter abbreviations are not used to begin a note." See also RDC Supplement 1949-51, p. 5, for additions and corrections.

II. Preliminary and other textual matter.

A. Forewords, prefaces, annotations, etc., in a typical bibliography are written formally, and with few abbreviations. However, various disciplines, notably those belonging to the fields of science, technology, and industry, have accepted certain standards for abbreviating words used in the text. Bibliographers whose work is addressed to specialists in these subjects should inform themselves of the conventions governing approved abbreviations. Otherwise, for a statement of considerations and examples applicable to the abbreviations to be used in the textual part of bibliographies see GPO, p. 141-154.

B. Bibliographical references, cited in the body of the text, retain the abbreviations usual in bibliographical entries, e.g., as in the following annotation:

> Contains in the form of a summary Lucia Moholy's article describing the Aslib Microfilm Service, published originally in the Journal of documentation, v. 2, Dec. 1946: 147-173.

C. Associations, agencies of the United States Government, and international organizations frequently are better known by their initials or abbreviations of their names than by their complete official designations, e.g., AAUW, FAO, FID, and NATO. If these familiar condensed or abbreviated names are in good taste because such short forms fit the style of a bibliography, it is entirely permissible to use them in annotations after the full form of the corporate name has first been used with initials, e. g., United Nations Educational, Scientific and Cultural Organization (UNESCO). A warning is also in order that such expressions are not thoroughly standardized, so that identical initials or abbreviations are assigned to different organizations by various authorities. Moreover, they pass out of common use, become unknown, and in a short time may cause confusion. In case of doubt, the full form is to be preferred in successive references.

ALPHABETIZING AND FILING.

Bibliographers are referred to the following source for guidance in alphabetizing and filing:

U. S. Library of Congress. Processing Dept. Filing manual. Washington, 1945. 1 v. (loose-leaf) Z696. U57
Documentation of these detailed rules is provided by abundant examples of their application. The section on "Corporate author" and that on "Place rangement" may be studied with special profit

NUMERALS. (RDC, Appendix IV; p. 129-130)

I. Bibliographical entries.

A. Substitution of arabic for roman numerals. Arabic numerals are substituted for roman, if it is possible, unless two numerals stand in such close relationship to each other that confusion results if the same style of notation is used for both, e. g., (National Arts Society. Publications, III, 2). However, numerals must be expressed as they are stated in the references cited, whether in roman or arabic notation, if they appear in author headings, titles of publications, quotations, and as references to pages, e. g., James II; The sad story of Maurice III; "The report covers chapters I-X of an earlier study made by the research staff"; see p. iii-ix.

B. Numerals spelled out or expressed in figures. "Arabic numerals are substituted for numerals that are spelled out if they occur elsewhere than in titles, in the names of corporate bodies, or in quoted matter."

C. Numerals at the beginning of notes are spelled out except in very unusual cases, e. g., First edition published June 1943.

D. Numerals in titles are retained as originally given in the title, whether expressed in figures or spelled out.

E. Inclusive numbering. References to inclusive pages are given in full, e.g., 210-219. The last number in inclusive reference numbers in an index is given as briefly as possible without being misleading, e.g., 10-15; 50-51; 98-101; 109-110; 200-210; 304-5; 412-16. The figures indicating the century in the last number in inclusive dates are omitted from the imprint unless the centuries are different, e.g., 1885-93, but 1899-1920. Inclusive dates in titles of publications are given as they appear on the title page.

F. Ordinal numerals. In English, ordinal numerals are written 1st, 2d, 3d, 4th, etc.; in foreign languages the form is 1., 2., 3., 4., etc.

G. Reference numbers. Whatever the arrangement of entries in a bibliography may be, whether alphabetical, chronological, or classified, all items are assigned arabic numbers, in numerical sequence from first to last, if the bibliography is to be indexed. Such numbering is designed to provide a direct method of locating each entry on its page, through the index.

II. Textual matter and annotations. When quantity, enumeration, measurement, and other concepts involving numbers must be expressed in the text (preface, introduction, annotations, etc.) accompanying a list of bibliographical entries, a question arises concerning the use of figures as opposed to spelling out numbers in words. The style to be followed under these circumstances is found in GPO, p. 155-160.

APPENDIX B

USE OF PRINTED CATALOG CARDS

The principles described in the manual are intended to guide bibliographers particularly in the preparation of references that are not represented by printed catalog cards, e. g., periodical articles and parts of series, documents, and other publications not analyzed in the catalog. Obviously, it is a great saving of time to the bibliographer if printed cards have been made for the publications he is citing because (1) the major problems of entry, as well as the subject headings, have been decided by the specialists in cataloging, and (2) duplicates of the cards may be used as copy for the typist. These duplicates may be obtained from the Card Division by use of the series number which is located in the lower right hand corner of the card. Unfortunately, the cards are sometimes not in stock and copies have to be made, preferably typewritten.

However, the compiler is warned that the printed cards must be edited carefully. Invariably the items assembled for a list include entries prepared in different years according to rules that differ from those currently used. This is especially true of capitalization, abbreviations, ellipses, imprint, series note, etc. In addition, entries for a bibliography do not need such details as size, subject tracings, etc.

Examples of printed catalog cards with editorial markings are shown below. Lines are drawn through parts to be omitted; double vertical lines direct attention to the inclusion of statements that might be overlooked otherwise; the indication of capitals and of other changes follow the proofreader's marks listed in GPO, p. 2-3.

Endo, Riuji, and

The Sinian and Cambrian ~~form~~ations and fossils of southern Manchoukuo, ~~by Riuji Endo ... and~~ Charles ~~Elmer~~ Resser. Mukden, Educational institute, South Manchuria ry. co., 1937.

~~1 p. l., ix,~~ 474 p. ~~1 l.~~ 73 pl. ~~(incl. fold. map) 26cm.~~ (Manchurian science museum. Bulletin 1)

~~Colophon in Japanese.~~
~~"Corrigenda" slip mounted on p. [2] of cover.~~
|| Bibliography: p. 367-369.

~~1. Geology—Manchuria. 2. Paleontology—Manchuria. I. Resser, Charles Elmer, 1889- joint author. II. Title.~~

~~41-11319~~

~~Library of Congress~~ Q105.M814, no. 1

~~[4]~~ ~~(507.4) 560.9518~~

Lovell, Eleanor ~~Cook~~

Index to handicrafts, modelmaking, ~~and~~ workshop projects~~, compiled by Eleanor Cook Lovell and~~ Ruth M~~ason~~ Hall. Boston, Faxon, 1936.

476 p. ~~23 cm.~~ (Useful reference series, no. 57)

Bibliography: p. 1–14.

——— ——— Supplement~~, compiled by Eleanor Cook Lovell and Ruth Mason Hall.~~ Boston, Faxon, 1943–

v. ~~23 cm.~~ (Useful reference series, no. 70, 79)

Includes bibliographies.

Z7911.L89 Suppl.

~~1. Handicraft—Indexes. 2. Models and modelmaking—Indexes. I. Hall, Ruth Mason, joint comp. II. Title: Workshop projects. (Series: Useful reference series, no. 57 [etc.])~~

Z7911.L89 ~~016.6~~ ~~36—27324*~~

~~Library of Congress~~ ~~[52r51c45]~~

Simmons, James S~~tevens, 1890–~~

Global epidemiology, a geography of disease and sanitation, ~~by James Stevens Simmons ... Tom F. Whayne ... Gaylord West Anderson ... Harold Maclachlan Horack ... and collaborators ...~~ Philadelphia, ~~[etc.] J. B.~~ Lippincott ~~company~~ [1944~~–~~]

~~v. maps. 26 cm.~~

"Material is based on surveys made for the Medical department of the United States Army ... The surveys ... represent the work of a large number of individuals associated ... with the Medical intelligence division of the office of the surgeon general of the United States Army."—Pref.

~~(Continued on next card)~~

~~S G 44—249~~

~~[52c3⅟2]~~

Simmons, James Stevens, 1890– Global epidemiology ... [1944– (Card 2)

Includes bibliographies.

~~CONTENTS.—v. 1. pt. 1. India and the Far East.—pt. 2. The Pacific area.~~

1. Epidemics. 2. Medical geography. I. Whayne, Tom French, 1905– joint author. II. Anderson, Gaylord West, 1901– joint author. III. Horack, Harold Maclachlan, 1912– joint author. IV. U. S. Surgeon-general's office. Preventive medicine service. V. Title.

RA651.S48 ~~614.42082~~ ~~S G 44—249~~

~~U. S. Army Medical Libr. for Library of Congress~~ ~~[52c3⅟2]~~

v. 13. Korea. Section 7: Agriculture.

U. S. *Army Service Forces.*
Civil affairs handbook. [Washington] 1944.
113 p. ~~v. in~~ illus., ~~maps. 26-36 x 50 cm.~~ (*Its* Army Service Forces manual, ~~M 350-~~M 370-7)

~~Some of the numbers issued also, under the same title, as Preliminary drafts by the Military Government Division of the Provost Marshal General's Bureau.~~
~~Includes bibliographies.~~
~~Consists of separate handbooks for 21 countries, issued in sections.~~

Selected list of sources: p. 110-112.

~~(Continued on next card)~~
~~46-16503*~~
~~[a49r47e1]~~

U. S. *Army Service Forces.* Civil affairs handbook. 1943- (Card 2)

CONTENTS.—[1] Albania. (M 362) v.—[2] Austria. (M 360) v.—[3] Belgium. (M 361) v.—[4] Bulgaria. (M 358) v.—[5] Denmark. (M 366) v.—[6] France. (M 352) v.—[7] French Indo-China. (M 359) v.—[8] Germany. (M 356) v.—[9] Greece. (M 351) v.—[10] Hungary. (M 369) v.—[11] Italy. (M 353) v.—[12] Japan. (M 354) v.—[13] Korea. (M 370) v.—[14] Manchuria. (M 367) v.—[15] Netherlands. (M 357) v.—[16] Norway. (M 350) v.—[17] Philippines. (M 365) v.—[18] Poland. (M 364) v.—[19] Rumania. (M 363) v.—[20] Thailand. (M 368) v.—[21] Yugoslavia. (M 355)

1. World War, 1939-1945—Occupied territories. I. Title. (Series)

UA25.A12, no. M370-7 ~~no. M350, etc.~~ ~~46-16503*~~
~~(355.8) 940.5337~~

~~Library of Congress~~ ~~[a49r47e1]~~

U. S. *Congress. House. Committee on Banking and Currency.*

National housing act amendment. Hearing ~~before the Committee on Banking and Currency, House of Representatives, Eighty third~~ 83d Congress, 1st session, on H. J. Res. 160, Joint resolution to amend section 2 (A) of the National housing act, as amended. Feb. 17, 1953. Washington, U. S. Govt. Print. Off., 1953.

~~iii~~, 43 p. ~~24 cm.~~
Jesse P. Wolcott, chairman.
~~1. Insurance, Credit. 2. Building—Repair and reconstruction.~~
~~I. Title.~~

HG9970.C65U56 1953 ~~*368.85 368.81~~ ~~53-60411~~

~~Library of Congress~~ ~~[3]~~

APPENDIX C

ANNOTATIONS

While many bibliographies rightly may be prepared without annotations, others require these additional elements for a variety of reasons, such as the following: (a) entries are not self-explanatory; (b) achievement of the complete purpose of the work requires interest supplied by annotations; and (c) the scope of the bibliography justifies time and effort involved in supplying annotations to aid potential users rapidly to assess the value of individual items.

Successful annotations are not evolved from the application of dogmatic rules. Instead, they reflect knowledge, judgment, awareness of relative importance, and good taste on the part of the person who writes them. The greater the bibliographer's mastery of the subjects concerned, the more latitude to which he is entitled in preparing his annotations. There are, however, degrees of excellence in the special skill required for writing satisfactory annotations. For that reason a section on annotations is provided to indicate material gleaned from the literature of the subject and to be used for purposes of orientation and review.

I. Sources consulted during the preparation of this section include the following:

Chemical abstracts. Directions for abstractors and section editors of Chemical abstracts. Columbus, American Chemical Society, Ohio State University, 1952. 46 p. QD9.C47 1952

Haines, Helen E. Living with books; the art of book selection. Columbia University Press, 1950. 610 p. (Columbia University studies in library service, no. 2) Z1003.H15 1950

McClelland, Ellwood H. Abstracts and annotations. Special libraries, v. 34, Sept. 1943: 363-372. Z671.S71, v. 34

Sayers, William C. Berwick. First steps in annotation in catalogues. 2d ed., rev. London, Association of Assistant Librarians, 1932. 12 p. Z695.S285

II. Checklist of specifications. When writing annotations the bibliographer will find it wise to keep before him a checklist of specifications from which to select those applicable to his work at a given time. The literature of annotating yields the following suggestions for such a list:

1. Avoid repetition of information already explicit in the entry being annotated.

2. If the authority of the author has a bearing on the usefulness of the work, give his title or state his experience.

3. Confine coverage of topics to those significant for the purpose of the bibliography and avoid the inclusion of extraneous ideas.

4. State the scope of the work, employing terminology susceptible to successful indexing in relation to the subject of the bibliography.

5. Give the author's central thesis if it is possible to do so in few words.

6. Explain qualifications requisite to the successful use of the item, e.g., knowledge of advanced mathematics, statistical analysis, theoretical economics, etc.

7. Indicate limits imposed by dates or periods covered.

8. Call attention to the individual slant of the book, if important, e.g., "Techniques described apply to microfilm made according to British standard specifications."

9. In exceptional cases that justify particular attention or involve conflicts of opinion quote from or cite an important review, abstract, or reply by a recognized authority.

10. Point out features of importance, such as documentary appendixes, indexes of sets, bibliographies, and extensive illustrative and graphic material.

11. Compare the work in question to another publication of similar or contrasting purpose, if such comparison is an aid in establishing scope and purpose.

12. Omit evaluation according to personal opinion of the bibliographer, but supply objective facts on which the user may base his own opinion.

13. Compress the annotation into the fewest possible words, considering 30 to 60 desirable and over 100 prohibitive unless a review, not an annotation, is called for.

14. Omit redundant annotations if the authority and importance of the work are obvious from the author and the title, e.g., in the case of historic documents, laws, treaties, etc.

15. Explain in the preface, and if necessary state in different words in a note at the beginning of the bibliography, any puzzling stylistic usages, and the omission of annotations, which might impress the user as an evidence of superficial treatment.

III. Style. Two clearly marked styles used in writing annotations represent the extremes of several choices open to the bibliographer. These are: (a) the conventional literary style; and (b) the clipped, telegraphic style. Both styles may be used in the same bibliography according to which is best suited to individual items.

A. Conventional style. Those who choose to annotate in this style must use the best possible idiomatic English in sentences that are clear, complete, and readable. An opening sentence expresses the principal point of the annotation, while transitional words and phrases lead on to other sentences embodying subsidiary ideas. A conclusion or climax of sorts then adds emphasis to a graceful and polished piece of writing. The peculiar virtue of this style, if its art has been thoroughly mastered, is that it lends itself to persuasive writing which helps to stimulate interest and fix attention. It is particularly well adapted to the annotation of books selected for complete reading. Works chosen not for thorough reading but for consultation in the course of study and research present a different problem and bring to light difficulties in the use of the conventional style. Quite justly the annotator may feel that he loses precious opportunities to present information useful to serious students, while he struggles to be urbane, elegant, and interesting in 30 to 60 words. He may decide, therefore, that the telegraphic style is the one best suited to his purpose.

B. Telegraphic style. When this style is followed, introductory words, phrases, and sentences are omitted. Articles, adjectives, and adverbs, when they are not essential to clarity of meaning, are dropped. Familiar abbreviations of technical bibliographical terms, e.g., bibl., p., v., cf., etc., legitimately may be employed. Elliptical expressions and compact phrases are substituted for complete sentences, while connective and transitional elements tend to be eliminated. Frequently no period appears until the end of the annotation is reached, although in such a case semicolons may be used between independent expressions within the annotation. While it is difficult to avoid the monotony that results from repeated use of nouns without verbs, and vice versa, which is an inevitable result when this style is used, at its best it produces a workmanlike effect, with a refreshing lack of ostentation. So brief and direct a presentation of essential facts may be welcome to specialists and scholars already thoroughly familiar with the trends in literature of a subject field.

IV. Form. An annotation, in the form of a paragraph, is placed after the main body of the entry in a bibliography, following the necessary supplementary notes. When space is at a premium in a long bibliography, it may even be necessary to coalesce notes and annotations in a single highly compact paragraph. In such a case, great care must be exercised to avoid confusion from compression that becomes cryptic.

V. Capitalization and punctuation. Rules governing the style of capitalization and punctuation used in annotations are found in GPO, p. 17-50, 127-139, with the exception that titles of publications to which reference is made in annotations are capitalized according to the rule given in this manual in the section on Capitalization. An abbreviation, e.g., "vol.," at the beginning of a note or annotation is capitalized.

VI. Rules of composition. The rules of English composition used in writing annotations in conventional style follow recommendations found in GPO, in which see particularly "Abbreviations," p. 141-154, and "Numerals," p. 155-160.

APPENDIX D

TITLE, PRELIMINARY MATTER, AND MAKEUP

A. Title. The importance of the title of a bibliography should not be overlooked. A concise, distinctive title beginning with the key words of the topic is easily remembered, easily filed, easily listed in other bibliographies, and easily found in a library catalog. Lengthy, detailed, all-explanatory titles and those beginning with such words as List, Bibliography, or Books should be avoided.

B. Title page. The title page of the bibliography should contain (1) the full title of the compilation, (2) the name of the compiler, (3) the issuing office, (4) place, and (5) date. The practice of the Library of Congress concerning authorship and statement of departmental and organizational units designated on title pages of its publications, with exceptions, are prescribed in its General Order No. 1542, February 10, 1954.

C. Verso of the title page. This should give the Library of Congress card number, and, in the case of a priced bibliography, a form statement regarding where and how it may be obtained.

D. Cover. Usually the cover contains the same information as the title page without the name of the compiler.

E. Preliminary statements. It is generally desirable to include some introductory notes to explain the scope, treatment, etc. The following statements are suggested but not all of them are always necessary:

1. The foreword "is an introductory note written as an endorsement by a person other than the author." (GPO, p. 11) In the Library of Congress this usually is written by the Chief of the Division or the Director of the Department.

2. The preface "states the origin, purpose, and scope of the work and sometimes contains acknowledgments of assistance." (American Library Association. Editorial Committee. Subcommittee on Library Terminology. A. L. A. Glossary of Library Terms, by Elizabeth H. Thompson, Chicago, 1943. p. 104. Z1006. A5) Acknowledgments "serve primarily to ascribe important substantive and editorial contributions . . . [but] routine assistance on the part of a member of the Library staff in line of duty should not be acknowledged" according to the Library's General Order No. 1542.

The following points which give an idea of what should be included in the preface, are copied from the Manual for Bibliographers in the Library of Congress (1944) p. 3.

(1) An exact description of the scope of the bibliography.
(2) A statement explaining its limitations and any omissions which are not obvious from the description of its scope.
(3) An account of the purpose of the bibliography, in terms of the group it is designed to serve and the type of use the group can or will make of it.
(4) A statement of the need for the bibliography in terms of the importance of the subject and the lack of other bibliographies in the field; the manner in which it supplements bibliographies in related fields.
(5) A justification of the selection of items in the case of a critical bibliography, with some explanation of the standards employed.
(6) An account of general characteristics of the text; i. e., the use of annotations, citations of reviews, etc.
(7) An explanation of any departures from the standard form of entries, or the omission of information usually included, or the addition of information not usually included.
(8) An explanation of the arrangement of entries and its justification in terms of the purpose of the bibliography, the nature of the material listed, etc.
(9) A description of the index or indexes.

3. The introduction discusses the subject and its treatment in the bibliography. (A. L. A. Glossary of Library Terms, p. 75)

4. The table of contents, prepared by the bibliographer, lists the preliminary matter, each section heading with its subsections, and page references. If the list is not to have an index, a detailed contents listing is desirable.

5. Key to symbols. If any symbols of outside libraries or of divisions within the Library of Congress have been used in the compilation, these are brought together and listed alphabetically with the names of the libraries represented.

If certain words, names of corporations, etc., have occurred so often in the bibliography that they have been abbreviated, they may be listed in the "Key to Symbols and Abbreviations."

F. Makeup. Generally the following order and paging is used. (Based on GPO, p. 10-12.)

1. Cover
2. Title page (with the verso of the title page these are considered to be roman numerals "i" and "ii" but they are not numbered on the sheet)

3. Contents)
4. Foreword)
5. Preface) small or small capital roman numerals
6. Introduction)
7. Key to symbols)

8. Bibliography)
9. Index) arabic numerals

However, if the preliminary matter is completed before the typing or printing of the bibliography is begun, continuous paging of 4-9 in arabic numerals is preferred.

APPENDIX E

PREPARATION OF THE INDEX

Unfortunately the technique of indexing bibliographies has not produced its own literature as the indexing of books has done; for this reason the bibliographer finds it necessary to adapt for his own requirements the principles of indexing textual matter. Publications useful for this purpose include the following:

Wheeler, Martha T. Indexing; principles, rules and examples. 4th ed. [Albany] University of the State of New York Press [1942] 76 p. (University of the State of New York bulletin, no. 1230)
Z695.9.N53 1942
Reading list on indexing: p. 68-70.

Brown, George E. Indexing, a handbook of instruction. London, Grafton; New York, H. W. Wilson, 1921. 137 p. (The Coptic series)
Z695.9.B87
Literature: p. 129-130.

Clarke, Archibald L. Manual of practical indexing, including arrangement of subject catalogues. 2d ed., rev. with numerous alterations and additions. London, Grafton, 1933. 276 p. Z695.9.C59 1933

Collison, Robert L. Indexes and indexing; a guide to the indexing of books, and collections of books, periodicals, music, gramophone records, films, and other material, with a reference section and suggestions for further reading. London, E. Benn, 1953. 155 p.
Z695.9.C63 1953

Crane, Evan J., and Charles L. Bernier. Indexing and index-searching. In Casey, Robert S., and James W. Perry, eds. Punched cards; their applications to science and industry. New York, Book Division, Reinhold, 1951. p. 331-350. Q180.A1C33
Supplementary reading: p. 348-349.

Haykin, David J. Subject headings; a practical guide. Washington, U.S. Govt. Print. Off., 1951. 140 p. Z695.H36
At head of title: The Library of Congress.

Neiman, Stella (Duff), and Lester J. Cappon. Comprehensive historical indexing: the Virginia gazette index. American archivist, v. 14, Oct. 1951: 291-304. CD3020. A45, v. 14

The preparation of a simple author index for a bibliography on a limited subject presents few difficult problems. With the addition of names of editors, compilers, and other persons mentioned in the entries, the list of author headings, when thrown into alphabetical arrangement, becomes the index. In the same way, a bibliography in chronological arrangement of a voluminous author's works is provided with an index after little more effort than that involved in copying and rearranging the titles that have already been recorded in the entries. It is a general index of authors, subjects, and significant titles, or a subject index of an extensive classified bibliography, that requires special effort on the part of the indexer.

In order to make the best use of the assets that exist it is necessary to plan the index with the same care that is applied to planning the bibliography itself. When the larger questions of the type of index to be used and the coverage to be made are settled, there remain smaller details of form, capitalization, punctuation and indention to be determined. Memory is not a safe guide in such matters, and a record should be kept of decisions made about them, to avoid later laborious corrections of inconsistencies.

It has been said that there is no such thing as a fairly good index. It is either excellent or poor; if poor, it is certainly inadequate and probably misleading. Professional indexers ascribe to a good index such significant characteristics as: (1) accuracy; (2) clarity; (3) sufficient fullness of coverage; (4) wisely chosen subject headings; (5) brevity; and (6) consistency. Indexes of bibliographies having these desirable qualities are prepared with the following points in mind:

1. Headings. The correctness and appropriateness of the headings provided in an index chiefly determine its usefulness in leading the reader to pertinent references. Personal and corporate authors are indexed under the form used in the bibliography itself, in order that identification through the index may be certain. Personal names of authors are inverted. Titles of publications are chosen for indexing on the basis of their distinctiveness or significance. Words such as "bibliography," "list," "catalog" at the beginning of titles usually disqualify the entry for indexing under title.

Knowledge of terminology that has been gained during the preparation of the bibliography provides the necessary technical background for selecting the subject headings and subheadings useful for characterizing the items included in the compilation. However, formal subject headings used in lists and catalogs should not be followed slavishly; since the aim is always to select the terms best known to potential users. These terms are not necessarily the ones to which bibliographers are conditioned by their work in libraries. It is also particularly important to select specific subject headings for books that deal with the specific subject, and to index general books under general headings. But if the index is a detailed one, and it is desired to relate specific and general subjects in order to give the maximum amount of direction by means of the index, the device of "duplicate entry" may be employed. Such entry simply implies repetition of the reference number under a second heading, e. g., "Communicable diseases, 29" [specific heading]; "Medicine and health, 5-17, 29" [general heading]. Obviously, since the general heading includes substantial additional references, a "see also" reference from the specific to the general subject is useful, e. g., "Communicable diseases, 29. See also Medicine and health."

Duplicate or even multiple entry may be made when there is reason to believe that several synonyms are used so widely by different groups to name the same subject that it may be known almost equally well by all of the terms. However, if numerous references are involved, repetiton makes the index cumbersome, so that choice of one specific term is preferred, with cross references from other terms. Even in the use of cross references the aim should be to avoid the necessity of numerous "see" references by selecting headings on the basis of careful analysis of the subject, in order to make them appropriate and explicit. When a main heading gathers to it so many subheadings that they are difficult to scan rapidly, it is probable that the subject requires further analysis and that several more specific headings should be used for different references at first placed under the same heading.

The subject of the bibliography itself is not ordinarily used as a subject entry in the index, since all items indexed relate to it.

2. Reference numbers. Since many entries may appear on one page of a published bibliography, it is usually desirable to assign a reference number to each entry, using an orderly progression from first to last, and to refer to these numbers in the index rather than to page numbers. If inclusive numbers are used, only the figures necessary to identify the second number are given, e. g., 208-9; 420-31; 193-201.

3. Cross references. The "see" cross reference is used when no item appears under a heading and the reader consequently must be referred to another heading. The "see also" cross reference suggests additional headings under which useful references may be found. Repetition of reference numbers under different headings (duplicate or multiple entry) is preferred to elaborate cross references when only a few entries are involved.

4. Inverted and uninverted subject headings. Three types of index headings deserve special mention: (a) the adjectival heading, consisting of a noun and its adjective; (b) the phrase heading, e. g., two nouns connected by a preposition or conjunction; and (c) the qualified heading in which a word is added to the entry word to limit its meaning. Adjectival headings may be uninverted or inverted according to their significance for the subject being indexed, e. g., National bibliography; Bibliography, national. The same rule holds true of phrase headings, e. g., Radio in navigation; Navigation, radio in. "See" references are provided from the uninverted to the inverted form and vice versa as required. The word used to qualify an entry word follows the latter and is enclosed in parentheses, e. g., Saad-Abad Pact (1937); Property (law).

5. Subheadings. A particular character or phase of a main heading is indicated by a subheading, also called a "modifier."

6. Style. The "line by line" or "tabulated" style of indexing is preferred to the paragraph style by numerous bibliographers. Following the former style, headings are arranged alphabetically, preferably in two columns on each page. Subheadings are indented a specified number of spaces to the right of the heading itself. They are entered individually on separate lines below the entry word, and are arranged in alphabetical, chronological, or logical order. Choice of the order to be followed is determined by its suitability to the subject being indexed.

7. Capitalization. The entry word of each heading is capitalized as well as the proper nouns and their derivatives in the remainder of the heading. Capitalization of additional words in foreign languages is supplied in accordance with the practice of the country. The entry word of a subheading is in lower case unless it is a proper noun or foreign word that requires capitalization. In a "see" or "see also" reference the first word following those references is capitalized, e. g., Towns. See Cities and towns. The inverted element in an adjectival or phrase heading is not capitalized unless it is the derivative of a proper noun or unless it involves the use of a foreign word capitalized in the language in which it is expressed. The first word and all important words in titles of publications listed in the index are capitalized (see page 30).

8. Abbreviations. Generally the abbreviations used in the index are those listed in Appendix III of Rules for Descriptive Cataloging in the Library of Congress, p. 121-127. However, if any uncertainty exists concerning the clarity of an abbreviation the word is spelled out.

9. Italics. Elements regularly italicized in the entries of the bibliography are italicized also in the index, e. g., subdivisions of corporate names; geographical location of corporate bodies supplied after their names; "see" and "see also" references; and explanatory terms following personal names, such as "ed.," "tr.," and "comp." Titles of separate publications listed in the index are italicized, and titles of articles, chapters of books, if listed, are enclosed in quotation marks.

10. Mechanics. Bringing an index into existence requires mechanical organization to produce a key to information and a reliable tool. To achieve these ends, some bibliographers prefer to work from the carbon copy of the bibliography supplied by the copyist. This manuscript is handled twice in the first operations of indexing. During a first and rapid review, author headings, personal names, significant titles, and key words in notes and annotations are underscored. The aim is, at the same time, to review the relation of the parts to the whole and to bring into sharper focus the requirements to be satisfied by the index.

After the step just described, the bibliographer makes a second examination of the manuscript. At this stage of the work the names and titles that are underscored are copied on 3x5 cards by the bibliographer or a clerical assistant. Each key word that constitutes a satisfactory subject heading at the same time is written on a separate card. If it is not adapted for this use, a synonym or subject heading in the bibliographer's list is substituted. Necessary subheadings are supplied and reference numbers are added to identify items indexed. The transcriber is warned against the false economy of trying to force numerous subheadings on one main entry card. Time spent in rewriting the main subject heading on a separate card for each subheading is regained in full when the index is finally edited. In the course of the operations just described, cross references are prepared. The alphabetizing of the index cards keeps pace with their preparation.

When the last item in the bibliography is indexed, the alphabetic file of index cards is edited. Subjects that show a confusing number of subheadings are analyzed further and divided more exactly if possible. Cross references are verified, rechecked, and supplemented at need. Cards for subheadings of each main subject that has been modified in this way are transferred to a unit card under the proper heading. At this time the subheadings are rearranged if an order other than alphabetical is desired. A spot check is made to verify the accuracy with which the reference numbers have been transcribed, and the index is ready for the copyist. Proofreading the copied index is the bibliographer's final responsibility for it.

Another method of indexing a bibliography is preferred by some bibliographers. It is that of indexing each entry when it is annotated, using notes taken for the purpose during the evaluation of the work. By this method the index builds up as the bibliography grows, while revisions and corrections are made as the necessity for these manifests itself. Reference numbers are added to the index cards after the bibliography has been copied. In all other respects, such as the use of 3x5 cards, alphabetizing, and the treatment of subheadings, the procedure is essentially the same as that used in the first method described.

By way of a reminder, it may be reiterated that the list of subject headings kept by the bibliographer as a guide to his search for desirable works to include in the bibliography, and the terminology he selects when writing his annotations go far to solving many problems of indexing. These points are more fully discussed in the sections of the manual devoted to Procedures and to Annotations.

APPENDIX F

BIBLIOGRAPHICAL PROCEDURES AND TECHNIQUES; A SELECTED LIST OF REFERENCES

1 American Institute of Physics. Style manual for guidance in the preparation of papers for journals published by the American Institute of Physics. New York, 1951. 28 p. QC28.A5
See particularly p. 5, 14-15.
See also "Magazine abbreviations for references": p. 16-18.

2 American Psychological Association. Council of Editors. Publication manual. Washington, American Psychological Association, 1952. 61 p. BF1.P75, v. 49, no. 4, pt. 2
Issued as a supplement of the Psychological bulletin, v. 49, no. 4, pt. 2, July 1952.

3 American Standards Association. Style manual for standards. [3d ed., rev.] New York (70 East 45th St.) 1949. 28 p. Z253.A68 1949
See particularly p. 12-14.

4 Appel, Livia. Bibliographical citation in the social sciences and the humanities; a handbook of style for authors, editors and students. 3d ed. Madison, University of Wisconsin Press, c1949. 32 p. Z1001.A64 1949
Previously published under title: Bibliographical citation in the social sciences; a handbook of style.

5 Barnard, Cyril C. Bibliographical citation. Librarian and book world, v. 39, May, July-Aug. 1950: 105-110; 171-175; 125-129[!] Z671.L63, v. 39
Emphasizes bibliographical style of citations in the field of medicine; includes references to articles and books on scientific bibliography; discusses abbreviations of titles of periodicals in bibliographical citations and gives 7 references on that subject.

6 British Standards Institution. Bibliographical references. London, 1950. 18 p. ([Report] British standard 1629: 1950) TA368.B8, no. 1629, 1950
Entries for references to patents are described on p. 6, 15-16.

7 Chicago. University. Press. A manual of style, containing typographical and other rules for authors, printers, and publishers, recommended by the University of Chicago Press, together with specimens of type. 11th rev. ed. Chicago, 1949. 497 p.
Z253.C57 1949

See Index under "Bibliography."

8 Fry, Bernard M. Library organization and management of technical reports literature. Washington, Catholic University of America Press, 1953. 140 p. (Catholic University of America. Studies in library science, no. 1) Z695.1.S3F7

9 Gatner, Elliott S. M., and Francesco Cordasco. Handbook for research and report writing. 2d ed. New York, Barnes&Noble, 1951. 142 p. (College outlines series, 78) LB2369.G3 1951

See particularly "Footnotes," "Documentation," and "Bibliography": p. 40-46.

10 Gibbs, Helen M. The research or technical report; a manual of style and procedure. San Francisco, Robert R. Gibson, 1950. 131 p.
PE1478.G5

See particularly "Bibliography and footnotes": p. 77-94.

11 Hendricks, King, and L. A. Stoddart. Technical writing. Logan, Utah State Agricultural College, 1948. 117 p. PE1478.H4 1948

Previously published under title: Utah State manual for research writing.

See "Bibliographical form in finished copy": p. 54-59.

12 Higgins, Marion V. Bibliography; a beginner's guide to the making, evaluation and use of bibliographies. New York, H. W. Wilson, 1941. 42 p. Z1001.H6

13 Hubbell, George S. Writing documented papers. 3d ed. New York, Barnes & Noble, c1951. 164 p. (College outline series, 37)
PE1478.H8 1951

14 Hurt, Peyton. Bibliography and footnotes; a style manual for college and university students. Rev. and enl. by Mary L. Hurt Richmond. Berkeley, University of California Press, 1949. 167 p.
Z1001.H95 1949

See p. 55-56 for a selected list intended to serve as a general guide to additional manuals of style and bibliographical form.

15 Iowa. State College of Agriculture and Mechanic Arts, Ames. Graduate College. Manual on thesis writing. 3d ed. Ames, 1951. 78 p. LB2369.I57 1951

See particularly the section on bibliography and footnotes, p. 18-27.

See also examples in Appendixes A and B, p. 42-50.

16 Joughin, George L. Basic reference forms; a guide to established practice in bibliography, quotations, footnotes, and thesis format. New York, Crofts, 1941. 94 p. PE1478.J6

Includes a section on special reference forms for use in the citation of legal, scientific, governmental, medical, engineering, and unpublished materials; not designed as a complete guide for specialists, but rather for undergraduate students and beginners in research work.

17 Kent, Sherman. Writing history. New York, Crofts, 1941. 136 p. D16.2.K45

See "Style and usage": p. 70-101.

18 Lester, John A. A guide to the preparation of research papers. Rev. ed. Haverford, Pa., Haverford College, 1949. 26 p. PE1478.L4 1949

See particularly "Forms of reference and documentation": p. 18-21, 25-26.

19 Leube, Sigrid, and Waldo Chamberlin. How to cite United Nations documents [in] footnotes [and] bibliographies. [New York, New York University, 1952?] 17 p. (New York University Conference on United Nations Documents, May 19, 1952. Paper no. 2) Mimeographed.

20 The MLA style sheet, compiled by William Riley Parker. PMLA; Publications of the Modern Language Association of America, v. 66, Apr. 1951: 3-31. PB6.M6, v. 66

Described as the more or less official style sheet for 46 journals; includes also directions for preparing manuscripts acceptably for any one of 32 additional journals. Reprint obtained from the Treasurer of the Association, 100 Washington Square East, New York, N. Y.; price 10 cents.

21 McGraw-Hill Publishing Company, inc. Typographical stylebook; prepared as a standard of usage and practice for the McGraw-Hill publications. New York, 1949. 127 p.

See particularly "References, footnotes, and other annotations": p. 94-96.

22 Moor, Carol C., and Waldo Chamberlin. How to use United Nations documents. New York, New York University Press, 1952. 26 p. (New York University. Libraries. Occasional papers, no. 1)
Z674.N47, no. 1

23 Nixon, Emily C., and Waldo Chamberlin. How to catalog United Nations documents. [New York, New York University, 1952? 47 l.] (New York University Conference on United Nations Documents, May 19, 1952. Paper no. 3) Mimeographed.

24 Preparing literature citations. AIBS bulletin, v. 2, Apr. 1952: 21-23.
Serials Division

Report by the A. I. B. S. Publications Committee of the American Institute of Biological Sciences (2101 Constitution Ave., Washington, D. C.) concerning preferred forms of references in biological publications.

25 Price, Miles O., and Harry Bitner. Effective legal research: a practical manual of law books and their use. New York, Prentice-Hall, 1953. 633 p.
Law

Chapter 32 on "Standard legal citation forms" is abridged from Mr. Price's A practical manual of standard legal citations (1950).
Law

26 Sharp, Eleanor. Stylebook of The Encyclopedia Americana. Chicago, Americana Corp., 1946. 259 p.
Z253.S5

See particularly "Bibliography": p. 26-33; "Titles of publications": p. 190-197; "References and records": p. 205-210.

A supplement (1952, 65 p.) incorporates revisions made since 1946.

27 Special Libraries Association. Science-Technology Group. Technical libraries: their organization and management. Lucille Jackson, editor. New York, Special Libraries Association, 1951. 202 p.
Z675.T3S64

28 Stanford University. Press. Publisher briefs author; a manual for Stanford authors. Stanford, Calif., 1951. 31 p.
PN160.S9

See particularly p. 14-15.

29 Trelease, Sam F. The scientific paper, how to prepare it, how to write it; a handbook for students and research workers in all branches of science. 2d ed. Baltimore, Williams & Wilkins, 1951. 163 p.
T11.T7 1951

Original text, by S. F. Trelease and E. S. Yule, published in 1925 under title: Preparation of scientific and technical papers. See particularly "Literature citations": p. 82-96.

30 A Uniform system of citation; form of citation and abbreviations. 8th ed. Cambridge, Mass., Harvard Law Review Association, 1949. 84 p.
Law

31 U. S. Armed Forces Medical Library. Library manual: R-R-6. Washington, 1952. 4 p.
Outlines policies and general procedures for the compilation of extensive bibliographies; omits details of bibliographical style.

32 U. S. Dept. of Agriculture. Library. Bibliographic style; a manual for use in the Division of Bibliography of the Library. Prepared under the direction of Margaret S. Bryant, chief, Division of Bibliography. Washington, U. S. Govt. Print. Off., 1951. 30 p. (U. S. Dept. of Agriculture. Bibliographical bulletin no. 16) Z1009. U57, no. 16
Z1001. U54 1951

33 U. S. Geological Survey. Suggestions to authors of papers submitted for publication by the United States Geological Survey, with directions to typists, by George McLane Wood. 4th ed., rev. and enl. by Bernard H. Lane. Washington, U. S. Govt. Print. Off., 1935. 126 p.
Z235. U55 1935
See particularly "Footnote and other citations": p. 16-30.

34 Wiley (John) and Sons, inc. Author's guide for preparing manuscript and handling proof. New York, 1950. 80 p. PN160. W5 1950
See particularly "Details of editorial style": p. 50-60.

35 Williams, Cecil B., and Allan H. Stevenson. A research manual for college studies and papers. Rev. ed. New York, Harper, 1951. 194 p.
LB2369. W5 1951
See particularly "Basic bibliography entry forms": p. 124-126, 133-138.

36 Wistar Institute of Anatomy and Biology, Philadelphia. Style brief; a guide for authors in preparing manuscripts and drawings for the most effective and economical method of publishing biological research. Prepared by the cooperative efforts of the editors of journals published in the Wistar Institute and the staff of the Wistar Institute Press. Philadelphia, Wistar Institute Press, 1934. 169 p. PN146. W5 1934
A more recent but briefer publication is the Institute's A guide for authors: the Wistar Institute journals [Philadelphia, n. d.] 8 p.

INDEX

A

Q

R

☆ U. S. GOVERNMENT PRINTING OFFICE : 1954 O - 298813